COMING TO LIFE

Coming to Life

The Emergence of Self
in the Human Life Cycle

James L. Doak

Blue Dolphin Publishing

For information, address:
Blue Dolphin Publishing, Inc.
P.O. Box 1908, Nevada City, CA 95959

ISBN: 0-931892-11-2

Second printing, January 1993

Library of Congress Cataloging-in-Publication Data

Doak, James L., 1945-
    Coming to life : the emergence of self in the human life cycle.

    1. Self-actualization (Psychology)   2. Self-perception.
3. Loss (Psychology)   I. Title.
BF637.S4D59   1987   155.2   87.15801
ISBN 0-931892-11-2

Printed in the United States of America by
Blue Dolphin Press, Inc., Grass Valley, California

5   4   3   2

In Memory of my Mother,

Lucille Venetta Doak

Acknowledgments

An author is a wordsmith who attempts the formidable task of committing life to paper in a way that will stir life in the reader. Part of this task consists of him/her serving as a conduit of sorts between his/her mentors and those the author wishes to inspire or teach. My mentors are many—as a book of this nature owes much of its inception to all the people who have touched my life. My father, mother, brother and sister, friends, teachers, students, trainees, and clients have given and continue to give me lessons in living. Many of these lessons are included in these pages.

More specifically I want to recognize my primary mentors in the field of psychology, especially Fritz Perls and Alexander Lowen, neither of whom I have met personally. Their teaching comes to me through their writing and from the first generation gestalt and bioenergetic therapists who had the good fortune of knowing them well.

My more personal appreciation for clinical training and the subsequent material in this book extends to the trainers at the Gestalt Institute of San Francisco. Cyndy Sheldon, Frank Rubenfeld and Abe Levitsky come most readily to mind, but the kindness, sensitivity and skill of each Institute member was important to me in beginning a new way of living and working.

As the trainers of the Gestalt Institute gave me a foundation as a Gestalt practitioner, Dick Olney and Cherie McCoy have helped me deepen that foundation and expand it to include a "body" orientation in the practice of psychotherapy. They were my mentors for a number of years, teaching me the fundamentals of a self-exploration process for which Dick has coined the name, Self-Acceptance Training. I am particularly grateful to Dick for introducing me to many of the ideas in this text. He is an important part of this book because his work has become such an important part of me.

Thus far my acknowledgments have focused on those who have been central to my having something to say. But an author must go beyond having something to say, and acquire some facility in saying it. A first-time author like myself often needs much bridling when putting pen to ideas and concepts. For offering evaluation and critique in the writing process, I wish to thank my readers LeeAnn Brook, Bob Bacon, Ginger Konvalin, Ron Riffel, and particularly Karen Baer. I also want to thank Paul Clemens, the editor of Blue Dolphin Publishing, for his English editing and wise counsel around the whole publishing process. Finally, thanks to Rhoda Moser for a timely title that felt just right.

There is one last group of people without whom the writing of this book would have been impossible. They are the people with whom I currently share my life—the ones with whom important concepts become a lively, living reality. Because each of them lives in contact with me they will (I hope) feel my appreciation without being named, but I must mention my wife Ginger and son David for special distinction. I am fortunate and appreciative to have them with me often in reality—and always in spirit—as we experience this amazing phenomenon called life.

J.D.

Contents

SECTION III   THE ROAD BACK TO THE SELF

SECTION IV   MERGING BEYOND THE SELF

Preface

Not long ago, during a fiddle lesson, my instructor commented casually that it is the rhythm, the pulse, that gives a piece of music its life. So it is in our day-to-day lives. The notes of a musical piece are analogous to each facet of our humanness. Once we become familiar with each note through awareness and practice, we are ready to experience and create a lively, full rhythm. Our whole life is a precious opportunity to rediscover the full range of music within each of us.

This book is about self-exploration. The impetus to write it came out of my teaching college-level classes in self-awareness and my involvement as a psychotherapist in a clinical practice. I have long wished for a book that would serve as an intellectual stimulant to complement the more experiential, visceral process that characterizes the self-exploration process as I practice it.

The following pages are the outcome of that desire and should be of use to anyone who is committed to greater self-knowledge and deeper human experience. The starting point for a richer, saner world lies within each of us and depends on our willingness to make our inward journey. It is my hope that this volume will serve the reader as a provocative catalyst toward that end.

The theme underlying "self-exploration" is that each of us, in the process of living, has lost important aspects of our humanness. Few people in modern life experience themselves fully, and to the degree that one is incomplete, one is incapable of being a full participant in life as it unfolds.

The beginning chapters of this volume focus on the process of self-loss. Chapter I offers a description of what is often lost in our journey through life. Subsequent chapters describe how the loss comes about, and when various aspects of our humanness are likely to thrive or languish.

Midway through the book I describe in detail some of the outcomes of self-loss. It is here that the common symptoms of depression and anxiety receive attention.

The third section describes our dilemma as adults as we try to accommodate the duality of holding onto our limited identity while letting go and expanding to allow for greater wholeness. This is a central issue in psychotherapy, and I discuss my own orientation to assisting clients in this important and difficult process.

The book's final chapters address the process of intimacy, merging, and commitment that naturally occur when a solid sense of self is established. The focus of this process begins with interpersonal connectedness, and, in later chapters, expands to include work and spiritual development.

SECTION I

PERSONAL LOSS

1
What is Lost?

In my years of practicing psychotherapy it has been a challenge for me to discover central themes which underlie the myriad of stated problems that accompany my clients as we begin the self-exploration process. The question has been, "What is basic to human suffering and dissatisfaction in symptoms as far ranging as loss of direction, compulsive habits, depression, anxiety, poor interpersonal relating and the frequent complaint of general lack of aliveness and a decrease in richness in living?"

Many of my colleagues and I share the view that there are three basic conditions that contribute to these and other kinds of emotional dysfunction. They are, broadly stated, a loss of self, a decided lack of self-acceptance and self-support, and a lack of personal integration.

A loss of self refers to absence of awareness. It can pertain to lost feeling capacity, limited perceptive ability or reduced physical sensation. It can also refer to limited awareness of options (the creative process), and limits around possible behavior. In addition to these internal losses in experiences many of us compound self-loss by losing our capacity for external awareness and allowing the world to affect our internal process. Both kinds of awareness loss have a profound effect on our ability to move toward a sense of well being.

The second condition, lack of self-acceptance and support, refers not to absence of self, but to self-judgment which interrupts personal experience. Awareness which is interrupted in this manner has little chance for deepening or completion, a process that is essential for our innate need for solidness and expansion.

The final phenomenon underlying dissatisfaction or dysfunction is the lack of personal integration. The differences in our inner and outer world must be brought together in some form. To the degree they are not, we will be confused, ambivalent, incomplete, and possibly immoblized.

With these three premises established, psychotherapy becomes a process of expanding self-awareness, establishing a greater sense of self-acceptance for what is known and what is discovered, and, finally, focusing on the unification of all that we are toward a sense of ease and gracefulness.

Although, as I practice it, therapy is not primarily an intellectual process, it can be useful to establish models as a structure or backdrop to the work itself. One of these models asks the question, "What have I lost?" Another way of putting this could be, "What of my original nature has been unduly repressed, or where am I underdeveloped in terms of the broad spectrum of human experience?" In this model we could envision beginning life "full of ourselves." This fullness would include sound health in mind and body, a sense of our own natural rhythm, physical awareness and a vast, uniquely varied potential for human experience.

As we journey through life, we always abandon some of our nature for the sake of our surrounding social order. We become socialized, which is an important process of containment and structuring. But socialization can be done in a way which extracts too heavy a price, the price of excessive self-loss and resultant reduction in aliveness.

Graphically this might be represented by Figure 1 in which the circle represents our wholeness, and the lines within depict human experience, behavior and potential. Loss of self-contact is illustrated in Figure 2 as we deny and eventually are not aware of forbidden feelings, thoughts and behaviors. One can envision the circle, our wholeness, becoming smaller and smaller until the sense of self is minimal as represented in Figure 3.

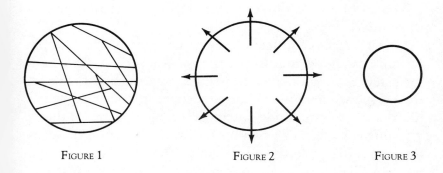

FIGURE 1   FIGURE 2   FIGURE 3

There are two results of such a process. The first is that, as we become smaller, we turn increasingly outward to become other directed. We conform, become addicted to approval, advice and direction, and become excessively reactive. We essentially see answers to life's riddles as "out there" and create lifestyles based on that formulation.

The second outcome from this process has to do with overidentification. Figure 3 represents what is left of us after self-reduction and, as such, can become our identity, our

sense of who we are—a limited sense to be sure, but at least a
kind of identity to which we cling. Thus if our intellect is
strong or has been encouraged over feeling and intuition,
we may overidentify with, and live life through, the medium
of rationality and ideas. Our self-concept will be more
"intellectual," and we will use it appropriately to add to our
lives and inappropriately to defend ourselves from others
and other forms of life within us. Someone limited to the
intellectual side of living will be seen at a party attempting to
turn gaiety into a philosophical discussion. In interpersonal
sharing when emotion is expressed, this type of person will
be unable to receive or share on an emotional level and may
respond with advice or teaching (both intellectual fuctions).
Silliness or whimsy is often avoided in themselves and in
others as being irrational, unpredictable, and, by implica-
tion, inferior.

I use "over-identification with intellect" as one example
of limited self-awareness, but the list could be endless. I am
the listener, the good one, the helpless one, the beauty queen,
the rock, the cutey pie or the challenger, to name a few. It's
not that there's anything untrue or wrong with any of these.
The difficulty comes when we begin to see ourselves as *just*
this or *just* that. We are more than we think, but to *know* that
we must begin to pay more attention. First we must pay
attention to *what is* left of us, what stances we allow, and
secondly to pay attention to what has been lost.

OUR LOSSES

Each time I have taught a class in self-awareness I have
asked participants to reflect on their own areas of under-
development or areas of human experience for which they

had little awareness or support. The following are the common themes that have evolved.

AFFECTIVE EXPERIENCE

Not surprisingly, the area of emotions is often one of the first categories addressed. The basic feelings of anger, fear, joy, sadness and sexuality are present in all of us in varying degrees, but in a culture which stresses rationality, productivity and control, few of us have escaped with a full capacity to feel deeply.

There are two major aspects to this area of loss. The first is the loss of the basic physical, visceral experience of feeling. In working with many clients in the initial stages of therapy, if I ask them how they feel, they will have little understanding of what I mean. If they do understand the question, they will often respond with a thought or the realization that they only vaguely have a sense of themselves on a body level. We seldom take the opportunity to focus on feeling in daily life, and to be with our sense of the moment.

The second aspect of feeling is whether or not, once the feeling is recognized, it will be expressed. Do we have the ability and the willingness to express, verbally and nonverbally, what emerges from within?

The loss of feeling and the option to express it is the beginning thread in this area of self-exploration. It is complicated in each individual by what kinds of feeling one allows, and in what manner or context one allows these feelings to be shared. For example, there are those who readily feel and express anger, but are slow to allow their longing for contact into conscious expression.

Roger, a client of mine, is a case in point. Severely abused by his stepfather, particularly when he was reaching for his mother, he became chronically angry. His anger soon colored much of his life and, as he came into adulthood, crowded out the softer emotion of desire for connectedness, a desire for connection that had once proved dangerous.

In this case Roger's limited sense of self (Figure 3) is that of an angry, mean, bitter man, and our task is to work through his defenses to rediscover the boy who reached for his mother out of his human wants and needs.

Other clients that I work with have difficulty allowing themselves the anger which is Roger's steady diet. Still others repress their fear, joy, excitement, sadness or sexuality. Aggressiveness is another affective experience that is diminished in many of us, but its opposite, passiveness/receptivity, is as likely to be absent.

I have listed the major affective experiences, the subtle variations on the themes are limitless, and thus, our affective life is open to endless possibilities. As we expand our awareness, we create a foundation for expressive movement, the next major area listed by my students in their discussion of underdeveloped experience.

PHYSICAL EXPRESSION AND MOVEMENT

Just as life is conducive to feeling, it is conducive to a full range of movement. Movement in many of us has been unnecessarily restricted. In therapy sessions and in classes one can witness censured movement in such basic expressions as dancing, playing, holding, touching, exploring, hiding, strutting, shouting, singing, laughing, smiling and crying.

As adults, few of us have a full ability to move gracefully and spontaneously, although we are charmed by the uninhibitedness of children in their movement.

Recently at an airport in Hawaii I felt this sense of charm when I watched a friend's daughter explore this new environment. Once in the terminal Meredith followed her curiosity with aggressive abandon, walking quickly from place to place and from stranger to stranger, as if she had much to do and see and needed to get on with it. Equally engaging for me were her parents' attitude and behavior. As time was available, one of them would simply "tail her" without verbal interruption, leaving her movement unhampered until there was a reason to break in.

In adult interaction we have lost much of our charm through restricted movement. If we are to regain mobility, it seems clear that we must travel backwards in time to rediscover our less restricted internal movement—feeling— and its partner, spontaneous action.

As I was walking to lunch with a male friend of mine last week, he put his arm though mine as we proceeded down the sidewalk, drawing me closer as he was telling me a story. Charming, simply charming.

THE USE OF OUR FIVE SENSES

Another area of frequent loss is our inability to make contact with the outside world. Fritz Perls, the founder of Gestalt Therapy, was fond of offering the following advice to his more cerebral clients: "Lose your mind and come to your senses." It is possible for us to increase direct contact with the world by increasing our attention to life as it is. We can figure out how life is; we can think through causality, hypothesize, theorize, plan and remember, all of which can add to our living, but Perls was reminding us not to overlook direct, uninterrupted experiencing.

The external part of this kind of experience comes to us, of course, through our vision, hearing, touch, smell and taste. This may be a meaningless concept at first, as we use our senses constantly to orient, but I believe Perls encouraged a deeper sense of receiving. For a variety of reasons many of us cut off full use of our vision. We may see some things, but close off to others. Our hearing may be similarly specialized, similarly underdeveloped, allowing in some stimulus but not listening to others. Touch, taste and smell follow suit. Impairment in any of our senses leaves us significantly self-encapsulated. Primarily, we *think* our way through life—without the rich *emerging* that takes place when we allow our inner being to be affected by our environment.

MODES OF CONSCIOUSNESS

Robert Ornstein writes extensively about two primary modes of consciousness in his book, *The Psychology of Consciousness* (1972). These modes are described broadly as intellect and intuition, and the primary theme of his volume is the importance of developing both for optimal human potential. The intellectual mode of consciousness refers to the rational, linear, analytic process which is so important in science, math, organization and productivity. It is the verbal, explicit, prediction-oriented part of our beings and attempts to give order and safety to our lives.

The intuitive side of our nature is more sensual, more wholistic, and less structured to time, place and person. It is more concerned with the total gestalt, and, as such, is more diffuse, less easy to put into words. This side of our nature connects us to our creativity, to spirituality, romance, mystery and magic.

Ornstein quotes Einstein who describes the interaction of the two sides of the brain as "combinatory play." Although each of us may have a constitutional predisposition to one mode of consciousness, each side enriches and supports the other. Everything in life is given depth by its polarity.

For example, in writing this book I began with a creative inspiration that came out of years of practicing therapy and teaching classes on self-awareness. The inspiration came from my intuitive sense of needing to express, to clarify and to be of use. Who I want to address through my writing and what I want to convey comes from the wholistic, experiential side of my being as I allow the concepts to emerge. In this phase, I may be more receptive, but my sense of self isn't easy to put into words. This side of experience is less articulate—more of a process of stirring, allowing, even waiting for concepts to form.

To move beyond the intuitive possibilities, however, takes positive action—the kind of support and purpose to which the intellect is best suited. What is my outline, what ideas follow, which lead, and which are irrelevant for a graceful, finished product? How can I organize my life to allow a space for this creative effort? What material and information is necessary to round out creative "hits." In short, how can my intellect provide the form in which my intuitive self can find expression?

If I have lost intellectual logical sharpness and development, much of my creative energy will lie fallow. Life will have the quality of bang, zoom, wow, gee, far out, out of sight: I will have many ideas, many intuitions, many ideas and feelings which don't become unified or deepened for completion, direction or progress. If on the other hand, I write with intellectual sharpness without intuitive inspiration, my writing begins to take on a technical, dry, mechanical style. It would be a writing without roundness, feeling and vitality.

Writing and life require both modes for completeness. Free flowingness and structure. Dreams and execution. Intuitiveness and rationality. Feeling and groundedness.

LIFESTYLE, POSSIBILITIES AND PERSONAL POTENTIAL

It is simple enough to begin exploring what one has lost as one's life journey has unfolded. Understanding what is absent is the obvious beginning point. But absence alone does not point to a need for change, for developing oneself in underdeveloped areas. It can, however, reflect an avoidance in one's potential for growth. It is an artful endeavor to know when a lack of feeling, behavior, skill or other personal pattern represents either stagnation or a blockage to growth, or when this lack is simply a result of one's core nature.

> Jim came into a therapy session wanting to look at his "blocks" in being more expressive at parties. As we worked with this issue, it became increasingly clear that Jim didn't inherently value much of party conversation, that he much preferred to be an observer at social functions. The work of our session then shifted to how he could support a more receptive stance when surrounded by others. How could he stop pressuring himself to create words when his natural bent was to be quiet?
>
> There was an interesting spinoff from this work that Jim shared with me months later. As he honored his right to not make conversation upon demand (his own or another's), he found that a new, more vocal part of himself emerged

occasionally. Several times in the current past he had found himself at parties being a veritable chatterbox out of a spontaneous, excited urge to express himself.

Another way to self-explore personal loss is to define what is "present"—what has received attention, become well developed, expressed and supported. After looking at what is present, one can readily examine the polar opposites. If a person is chronically busy, filling every moment, where have they relegated empty space? The reverse is a person whose days are an open sea of unstructuredness. Can the basically serious person begin to play with lightness? The talkative person with receptiveness? The slow person with swiftness? The responder with initiation? Can the city lover begin to include country life and vice versa? The safety-oriented woman allow herself an occasional adventure? The giver begin to allow—or experience—how to receive?

Questions of this nature are endless, particularly as we become more sensitive to the endless variety of human experience. These questions and others are just the beginning of the self-exploration process, a beginning query as to who we are, what has survived, and what has thrived in this complex path of becoming.

2

The Mechanics of Loss

Both socialization and the process of self-reduction described in the last chapter are based on our need for, and dependency on, "important others" during our developmental years. The socialization process is distinguished from self-reduction, however, by its positive intent. When we set out to "socialize" a child, we are doing so to enable him/her to satisfy a basic human need of community inclusion. We teach the person to contain, not destroy, feelings and impulses, to allow for more graceful, effective, cooperative interpersonal interaction. Hopefully this maturation process enriches the soul as opposed to bankrupting it.

Self-reduction, as used here, lacks the positive intent and design of socialization. It is not based on the child's need, but the parent's. In and of itself, asking a child to accommodate a parent's lack of tolerance is not self-damaging, but what IS harmful is making a child feel his/her behavior is wrong as a means of controlling him/her.

Recently on the tennis court my fifteen-year-old son, David, has had a problem with self-criticism and some verbal explosiveness. A temptation for me has been "to get on him," especially when I feel embarrassed about what others in the tennis club might think. Containing that desire, I have been able to honor my discomfort by telling him when it becomes significant, and indicate to him that I would need to stop playing if he cannot contain or shift his self-pressuring.

Allowing him his process without disowning mine has left David room to look at his own performance expectations. He does not need to defend himself, as there is no one attacking him. We can then discuss his process and attempt to understand it when the heat is off and we are off the court. His process is not life-enhancing and he knows it, but it would compound his dilemma to make him wrong for having strong feelings. I do not try to make him feel guilty, but help him become more self-aware of how he creates internal tension.

INTROJECTION

Most of our parents, because of their own upbringing, have made us feel wrong countless of times in subtle and not so subtle ways. Most often, with positive intent, they made us "wrong" by asking us to swallow whole their way of viewing the world.

The shoulds begin early and often have little congruence with what the child senses his needs to be. Eventually a soul is worn down. The child's confidence is depleted by external authorities whose judgments set in, eroding his own clear identity and opening him to adult conquistadors who take over the territory. The surrender is abject at first and forgotten later. So the foreign body rules, keeping the person ill at ease, suspicious of deviations or unexpected arousals, thwarted every time his second-hand value system proves unresponsive to his current needs (Polster & Polster, 1972).

The above quotation is a succinct description of the process of introjection, a major contributor to self-loss. Introjection is the swallowing whole of ideas, shoulds, attitudes, rules, mannerisms and perceptions without true assimilation and integration. It is antithetical to a process of allowing a child to take in, question, stir around and chew on new experience and ideas as he/she makes them his/her own in a unique assimilation.

Given enough pressure to conform, children will often succumb to being a passive swallower. They will be full of the second-hand value system Polster describes. In essence these children are full of other people's ideas and ideals with little room for, or a sense of, their own unique beliefs, style or creativity. When introjectors say "I think," they usually mean "They think," and their expression rings hollow. It doesn't have impact because it is a kind of parroting of other people's ideas, prejudices, direction and life style. Their statements lack originality, as the swallower (introjector) takes in, but fails to destructure the introject through critical examination. He then spits it back into the world in the same form. What was taken in does not become a part of the individual, and what comes out has little impact on anyone else.

In our age of experts and mass media, introjection has fertile ground. If one doesn't have an opinion and doesn't want to struggle to arrive at one, someone will feed you one ready-made. The difficulty with such an arrangement is that, in a world full of introjectors, we soon become bored. There is very little variance or personalization in conversation, very little spark in social interaction. What may have started out as an attempt to reduce pressure or maintain contact or identity with an autonomy-crushing parent results in a living deadness.

The insidious part of the introjection process is a key phrase in Polster's quote: "The surrender is abject at first and *forgotten* later." We have forgotten that we were conquered, and take for granted that our unexamined self is a true representation of who we are. Introjection has a firm foothold in our lives because it is often veiled as "common sense, science, psychic health, normality or public opinion" (Fromm, 1941). Fromm in his book, *Escape from Freedom*, describes this dilemma clearly when he writes:

> Most people are convinced that as long as they are not overtly forced to do something by an outside power, their decisions are theirs, and if they want something it is they who want it. But this is one of the great illusions we have about ourselves. . . . We have succeeded in persuading ourselves that it is we who have made the decision, whereas we have actually conformed with expectations of others, driven by the fear of isolation and by more direct threats to our life, freedom and comfort (p. 200).

In the past week of clinical practice I have worked with clients around introjected "shoulds" that interfered with experiencing sensitivity, asking for direction, a desire to punish, dependency, merging, pleasing others, fear and its expression, initiation, playfulness, importance and super-fluousness. This is but a partial list of human experiences that are repressed because we were taught to turn against them as inferior.

Thus far we have focused on rules and expectations as introjects, but in most of us there is an even greater self-damager—introjects around self-perception and attitude. When children have been criticized, hated, humiliated, and pressured consistently, they will internalize each experience respectively as self-criticism, self-hatred, self-humiliation, and self-demandingness. We do to ourselves what others have done to us.

> Janet, a client with whom I'd been working for a year, began to feel increasingly uncomfortable with me from week to week. Some of this she attributed to injunctions against positive feelings that were emerging toward me (introjects interrupting appreciation and warmth), but the intensity of the discomfort went deeper than that. Her words for the feeling were, "I'm not good enough for you." The physical sensation was that of shame.
>
> But shame for what? As she focused on her feeling, it came to her: "I'm not good enough because I'm a woman and you're a man." Raised in a family of all girls, Janet was in constant competition for the one male, a father who judged women as inferior. To maintain her connection with him she surrendered to his assessment, swallowing the notion that females are inferior to males.

Recognizing one's introjects is an important beginning. For Janet it means going from an undefined anxiety to sitting in the middle of shaming herself or elevating me. One can imagine how such a "conscious" experience might allow shifts to take place.

PROJECTION

Projection is the companion of introjection. Introjection is the taking in whole what is naturally the property of others. Projection is the process of giving others that which is naturally ours. In the former we are defining who we are without closely examining ourselves. In the latter we are defining who we are *not* to escape what we judge as undesirable. Introjection and projection are companions in the sense that with each introject, each should, rule or anti-self attitude, the introjector is likely to disown and project the undesirable trait. Thus the introject, "children should be seen and not heard," is followed by disownership or lack of awareness of a desire to express one's self. Projected onto the world, "they" (the outside world) become *the talkers*, and the child in social interaction becomes the listener. If one is taught to curtail curiosity through injunctions not to stare or to mind one's own business, the child may cease to use his eyes in exploration. The world then becomes the "big eye"—having all the looking power—and one feels under intense scrutiny. Sexuality is another human experience that is repressed and projected outside the self. When this is done, the world can become hypersexual, and one can become excessively uncomfortable with another's sexual feelings.

Sandra had been in therapy with me for about six weeks when she became anxious in my presence and perceived I was "coming on to her." I asked her to examine this perception more closely, for although I am attracted to some of my clients, I do not act on such feelings out of client respect and professional ethics.

As she focused on our interaction, it became clearer that *she* was feeling attracted to me, and was beginning to become seductive. Once her projection was recognized, she was able to enjoy her own feeling and reclaim the pleasure that is inherent in male-female energy.

Finally, aggression deserves special attention when we discuss the process of projection. Many of us have been overpowered in our developmental process by a power-hungry parent and have had little opportunity to exercise natural aggressive impulses. If we project our aggression out to the world, it becomes a powerful force which we fear, avoid and secretly hate. Perls used to be fond of saying that excessive fear of attack/aggression was a reflection of an individual's disowned desire to attack/aggress.

> Dick, a man who was treated sadistically by his father in his youth, was mildly paranoid and moderately fearful of humiliation in social interaction. In many public gatherings he would become tongue-tied as he felt his body tense as if an attack was imminent.
>
> Being attacked is always a life possibility, but in neurotic fear one *expects* to get attacked and is frequently mobilizing energy unnecessarily to meet it. Dick *had been* attacked and *had been* humiliated. Neurotic fear is based on what has already happened, but a person who suffers from it is pretending that the same situation continues to exist (in this case that he has a father who will sadistically abuse him). Most importantly, the person pretends that he doesn't have the aggression (this he projects) necessary to deal with an attack should it occur.

Like its partner introjection, projection is sometimes difficult to ferret out. Both are defenses against our true nature and will become conscious only as one is ready for greater self-truth. We do have tools to use for the explorations however, and they are invaluable for discovering personal artifacts which are ready for the light of day. One of these is the statement, "We do for others what we want for ourselves." This statement describes the projective process in the following ways. If one characteristically is a helper, it could be that he projects his own desire to be helped. If so, the world will be seen through "help" colored glasses, and sometimes a person will "see" a need for help where it doesn't truly exist. The same could be said of the chronic protector. Is he unable to experience his desire for protection? Or is the challenger needing to be confronted and challenged? A client of mine challenged others frequently, for their benefit and hers, but rarely allowed another to challenge her.

> I have a pattern of challenging my close friends not to hold back from discovering what they love and moving toward it. At times this kind of encouragement can take on an aura of pressure, as I become heavily invested in rescuing them from passiveness and inactivity. At those times it often behooves me to look at my own need to be challenged. Where do I continue to hold back? Who or what do I love, and how am I including the loved person, activity or object in my life?

Another tool to use in defining projections is the statement, "We criticize in others what we disown in ourselves." If there is a full range of human potential within each of us and we are in touch with it, we will recognize *ourselves* in many of the actions human beings manifest. We may not be murderers, but we can understand murderous feelings and the desire to kill. We may not have an affair, but we are acquainted with our lust, passion and moments of abandonment.

When we are particularly self-righteous and condemnatory, it might behoove us to look at our own behavior or feelings around the area of disdain. Does my jealousy and suspicion of my partner reflect my own desire to wander? Does my criticism of the loud mouth at a party represent my own desire to be center stage? Does someone's childishness offend me because I know so little about my own youthful impulses?

As people begin to examine their projections, attitudes toward others often soften. Complaints lose a lot of their energy and bite as people recognize themselves in others. It doesn't mean that I will stay in contact with the loud mouth, the childish person, or the constantly angry individual, but I will not separate myself from them in my inner attitude. I, in essence, say, "Yes, I know that stance." The feeling of "I've been there" is a binding, merging phenomenon in relationships, and is one of the benefits of bringing back to self what is rightfully ours.

The other benefit of reowning projections is the renewed and expanded experience that can come. Clients frequently come into therapy with the complaint that no one seems to care. Although this may be true, a richness and infinitely more powerful focus can be had if non-caring is treated as a projection. How caring are my clients? Who do they care about and how would they describe this caring specifically? If their own caring, loving, listening, and accepting is limited, they have identified an area for expansion, a focus which can lead to greater aliveness and feeling. It may even lead to others caring more, but if the problem stays defined as "others don't care for me," potential for change is limited. It requires someone else to change, which often is a dead-end street.

3

The Developmental Perspective of Loss

"You are the sum total of all your yesterdays," was a favorite expression of my high school sociology teacher, Mr. Hillis. Although biased toward nurture in the nature/nurture controversy, he was encouraging us to look at the influence of experience on our personal development and organization, and hinting that all these experiences were embodied in our sense of self. Al Lowen, the founder of bioenergetics, makes a similiar point when he writes, "The person's history explains his behavior. I would make the general statement that no person can understand his behavior if he doesn't know his history. Thus one of the main tasks of every therapy is to elucidate the patient's life experience" (Lowen, 1975.)

The most senseless behavior can be understood if one knows the context (history) from which it springs. Each day in my office, clients exhibit behaviors which don't make any sense in terms of the immediate present or their lives outside the therapy hour. They will be frightened when they are safe, withholding when they have an urge to give, or giving when they wish to contain. So we must go to history, as it is to history that they are responding.

Bandler and Grinder (1979) present a useful metaphor for this interactive process:

> The basic use of analysis in face to face communication is the feedback loop. For example, if you were given the task of describing an interaction between a cat and a dog, you might make entries like: "Cat spits . . . dog bares teeth . . . cat arches back . . . dog barks . . . cat . . ."
>
> At least as important as the particular actions described, is the sequence in which they occur. And to some extent, any particular behavior by the cat becomes understandable only in the context of the dog's behavior. If for some reason your observations were restricted to just the cat, you would be challenged by the task of reconstructing what the cat was interacting with. The cat's behavior is much more difficult to understand in isolation.

In this metaphor the cat represents any one of us, while the dog represents the history that made irrational behavior rational, and meaningful. The therapist helps the client identify the patterns of the client's current life that are tied to historical experience. This is a beginning step in breaking the patterns that work against overall well being. To do this well a therapist must be grounded in how individuals come to be. With this knowledge he can identify together with the client what developmental tasks have been accomplished and where development has been impeded.

Developmental theorists like Sigmund Freud, and the neo-Freudians, Alfred Adler, Wilhelm Reich, and Karen Horney, have offered an invaluable structure for understanding and exploring the etiology of human behavior. However, I most often turn to two other psychoanalytic descendants in analyzing and understanding human character. They are Erik Erikson, who has made a major contribution to developmental understanding through his writing on the

Eight Stages of Man—see his *Childhood and Society* (1950); and Alexander Lowen, who synthesized Wilhelm Reich's work into character types—see Lowen's *Pleasure* (1975), *Betrayal of the Body* (1967), *Depression and the Body* (1972), *The Language of the Body* (1958), and particularly *Bioenergetics* (1975).

Both Erikson and Lowen have focused on tasks that need to be accomplished for optimal health during the maturation process. These tasks represent existential issues that, if adequately resolved, lead to an adult who is capable of intrapersonal and interpersonal aliveness. Each task has an optimal time for resolution, although any issue can be re-examined for greater resolution with or without professional help. In the truest sense, of course, life's core issues never get permanently resolved. They arise again in times of stress to be worked with consciously and unconsciously as we deepen our internal wisdom through learning life's underlying lessons.

THE ISSUE OF EXISTENCE

The first lesson comes as the infant makes the transition from the womb to the outside world. Our vulnerability at this stage is paramount. We are at the mercy of those around us and their good will. We will return to this kind of vulnerability only at times of crisis, when our ability to cope emotionally and physically is taxed beyond our capacity. In the end our death, and the deaths of those we love, will remind us of how vulnerable we truly are, but we know this only at a preverbal level at our life's beginning. *In utero* and in the months following birth, we are faced with *survival and our own existence as the tasks to be resolved.*

First impressions are powerful as we approach new experience. So it is as we come into life and experience how, at a precognitive level, we are received. The question to be answered at this level of development is, "Is there room for me, am I welcome?" At an even deeper level, "Do I have the right to exist?" The answer first comes from surrounding caretakers through their responses. Perceived acceptance, love and protection help the infant to internalize an affirmative answer to these questions. A negative answer has its roots in the infant's perception of chaos, fear and rejection.

Each of us has made some form of resolution around this issue. Resolved positively, we have an assurance that our existence, in and of itself, is proof of our right to take our place. Because deep within us we feel our birthright, we do not easily feel threatened by life, and our survival is not easily called into question. Resolved negatively, however, we could spend an inordinate amount of time and energy trying to attain elusive safety. We will watch for the threat from outside while we defend against the deeper threat that comes from within. I say "deeper threat" because it is our feelings of fear and anger that are the most ominous. We were (and are) fearful at the lack of support that greeted our entrance into the world. We were (and are) angry at those who could not respond or who responded to us with their own anger, coldness or rejection.

Those early feelings have long since been defended against, however, as no one can stay with the intensity that such vulnerability produces. To stay with one's fear or anger at that level would lead to overload, which could lead to psychosis. To prevent the disintegration in such an experience, the infant learns how to cut himself off from most bodily sensation. He ceases to exist on a body level and relies almost soley on thought for direction and a sense of self. He

has been overwhelmed by feeling and has made an unconscious decision to live without it.

Externally, the person who has not internalized his right
to exist (has not been granted permission) appears haunted
and somewhat vacant. It is as though he is not really present.
He doesn't take up space, often seeming to wait for another
to give him room (permission to *be*).

> Laurie frequently evidenced an apologetic manner in
> therapy sessions. She was sorry for being late, sorry for being
> early, sorry for knocking on my door, sorry for not letting
> me know she had arrived. She was sorry for telling me
> something or sorry that she withheld other things. Sorry,
> sorry, sorry. . . .
>
> As we focused on her apologetic nature during one of our
> sessions, I asked her to begin sentences with "Excuse me
> for. . . ." Shortly she burst forth with, "Well, excuse me
> for living," a sentence which went straight to the heart of the
> matter. Expressing this several times, her underlying, biting
> anger began to rise—anger at those (including herself) who
> refused to acknowledge and support her existence.

Without a sense of the body, Laurie and others like her
are left with *thinking* as a basis for their identity. This is a
tenuous basis at best because thought ungrounded in feeling
tends to run rampant. An individual can think anything, but
reality testing and stability come through use of the body's
sensation and its senses. Without this grounding, psychotic
process is always a possibility, even a likelihood, if the
person's disembodiment is severe enough. It is ironic that
reducing contact with the body, originally done to prevent
overwhelming feeling and insanity, may contribute to the
development of psychosis in the long run.

THE ISSUE OF NEED

When we carry within us our right to take our place on earth, we are free to turn our energy to issues beyond basic survival. We are free to experience our basic human needs as they emerge, and make attempts to have them fulfilled. In infancy this is a process between parent and child, which gives the infant a rudimentary sense of how the world, as represented by his caretakers, will respond to his basic rhythms. The first issue of life can be framed, "Do I have the right to be here?" The second issue to resolve is, "Do I have the right to make demands on my environment and have my comfort supported?"

Pleasure and satisfaction often refer to the experience that accompanies a reduction of desire (Houston, 1979), and it is particularly with our mother in infancy that we begin to develop an orientation toward our desire or need and its resolution. A loving mother honors our rhythms around hunger, elimination, warmth, touch, continuity and connection in such a way that we begin to trust the world (and eventually ourselves) in a very deep way. We incorporate our mother's acceptance of our needs into a lifelong pattern of seeing need and nature in us, and naturally responding to desire in a way which fulfills. Eventually, when we grow beyond childhood's self-centeredness, we will extend this orientation to those around us.

In addition to this supportive organization around need, a loving mother or father will promote a deep regard for interpersonal connectedness—at base an appreciation for physical closeness, merging and love. Elizabeth Kubler Ross has said that mothers should be pillows for their dying children. I extended that poignant image to include all mothers and all children. Taken further, we could make the broad statement that all of us could be pillows for anyone to land on. The roots of our willingness and desire to be a pillow, or to be pillowed, are in these early, open-hearted times, as we get acquainted with the outside world.

Subtle or blatant disregard for our needs at this time, as reflected in our parents' frequent irritation, unresponsiveness, distance or abandonment of us, also leaves its mark. When those outside us are in any way against our needs, actively or passively we will begin the process of turning away from them as well. The result involves two primary feelings which can color a lifetime of experience.

The first is deprivation. If in our first experience around need we were deprived, this will often stay in the foreground in spite of later abundance. People who experience themselves as deprived will constantly look to the outside, the outer world, to satisfy that perceived lack. Their view is that they are not enough, that they must get more, that others are lucky, and they are not. Interpersonally, such a person will often be demanding and need strong reassurance, support and closeness because of a strong sense of vulnerability and a strong fear of abandonment.

In conjunction with this sense of deprivation is a strong orientation of mistrust. Ironically, the very world upon which this person relies so heavily is the same world in which they have very little faith. They look to others for life's essence, at the same time doubting that they will be given anything. The result is a half-hearted wanting and reaching out, with a subsequent collapse—a despairing withdrawal and frequent depression. Interacting with the world to have one's needs met requires a sense of that need, an aggressive, internalized right to have it met, and a faith that the world will frequently respond positively (or will at least not capriciously negate or ignore the need expressed). In the

early deprivation described above, none of these three
conditions have had a chance to develop, and the natural
flow of need and need fulfillment is weakened.

> Lisa came into therapy with the problem of an unsatisfac-
> tory relationship with her fiance. He was, according to her,
> emotionally withdrawn, and she found herself increasingly
> angry at his lack of availability. This kind of complaint would
> often lend itself to relationship counseling, but Lisa was a
> psychotherapist herself, and astute enough to know that her
> fiance's withdrawal was a secondary issue.
>
> The primary source of her dissatisfaction stemmed from
> her own early maternal deprivation. Deeply disappointed in
> her mother's lack of positive response to her needs, Lisa
> carried this unfinished gestalt into all intimate relationships.

We organize around our parents in a prototypical manner which becomes our core. If our first relationship (maternal) was one of deprivation, we will often recreate that
relationship (maternal deprivation) throughout life. *It's what
we know.* One way Lisa kept her sense of herself (deprived
child) was to choose depriving men. There are many other
ways that she maintained a sense of deprivation in her world,
and part of my task was to become familiar with that process.

THE ISSUE OF SEPARATENESS, THE RUDIMENTARY "I"

To go beyond the magic time of symbiotic love and
automatic need fulfillment, we must have an opportunity to fully experience that gestalt and be allowed to move on
beyond it. Disruption at any point in the maturational
process is the result of deprivation or excessive indulgence.
At this level excessive indulgence is the result of parents
being available for the needs of the child during infancy, but

unwilling to allow the separation process that begins the second and third year of life.

We can disrupt a child's reach for autonomy by holding him to a previous level of development, i.e. infantalize him/her, by actively squashing independent movement, or by covertly or overtly threatening a child's individuation with consequent withdrawal or abandonment. Each of these strategies is reflective of the caretaker's discomfort with separation, difference and distance, and, to the degree that these issues exist, will play a major role in the resolution of initial self-definition.

Physical maturation alone lends itself to an increased sense of self, as we begin to feel the potency that accompanies focused, directed muscle coordination in mobility, sound production, environmental manipulation and bowel and bladder control. Combine this with the brain's maturation in perception and conception, and the stage is set for a boundary to develop where merging was once the only possibility.

From within, then, we are receiving new stimuli which we use for formulating external awareness and awareness of the self. Interpersonally, this process is sharpened as we begin to differentiate ourselves from others. We do this often by negating, using the word "no." ("No, I won't; no, I don't want it; no, don't push me.") Saying no is a primary way to separate. To say, "No, I'm not like that," or "No, I'm not like you. I'm different—Don't assume with me, take time to know me as separate from your projections." This is the part in all of us that doesn't want to excessively merge with others and their rules, expectations, life scenarios and scripts.

If we were lucky, our autonomy was fostered by parents who socialized us in a way that allowed us to grow without needless self-censure. If our autonomy was crushed or discouraged, however, a lack of solid individuation is the result, and we may have symptoms as far ranging as hypervigilance (in the extreme, paranoia), passivity, passive-aggressiveness, chronic immobility or excessive ambivalence around intimate relating.

>   Anita was very careful in all of our sessions to take the lead. She was bright and used her brightness to quickly analyze and gain intellectual insight. There was a vigilance to her manner in our time together, and she recognized it when I brought it to her attention. It was a familiar stance to her.
>   As we explored her vigilance, she became aware of her fear of humiliation. She had been humiliated as a child around any failure to meet parental expectations, and her current vigilant control of herself and others was an attempt to avoid a reoccurence of her painful embarassment.
>   Ironically, Anita's excessive control is based on her belief that if others step into her world she will have a dangerous lack of control. For instance, if she allows silence in our session, I may offer her a self-exploration exercise that she couldn't support refusing. If she did such an exercise she might fail to do it "right," and would then be subject to ridicule. Finally, such an exercise might lead to discovering characteristics which could run counter to acceptable standards (parental introjections).

The parent who capriciously opposes their child's autonomy delivers the message, "It's either you or me." There is little room for difference—for an attitude of "you and me." The dilemma for the child is, "If I honor my direction, I risk losing you (the parent)." "If I give myself up, I can insure connection." Anita chose the latter resolution, internalizing her parents' demanding "shoulds." In our therapy sessions it was not my pressure to do gestalt exercises that she was guarding against. I have tremendous respect for my client's autonomy. She was guarding against her self-demands.

Demands to perform. Demands to cooperate. Demands to achieve. Demands to be a good girl.

Ironically, those of us who have avoided resolving the autonomy issue by swallowing another's rigid code, seldom achieve the high standards that our introjected parents command. We are angry at being victimized, and the humiliated victim within us opposes the arbitrary, unexamined code. The result is frequent "stuckness," as strong shoulds oppose strong rebellion. In this internal war self-pressure is pitted against procrastination, forgetfulness, and retentiveness. This kind of impasse is extremely frustrating, as energy is tied up and the individual is not free to move outward toward the world.

Imagining the conflict described above, one gets the sense of tremendous energy that could come forward in so many forms, and it is just this energy that is feared by the person housing it. These individuals have been humiliated and ridiculed frequently around their desires, directions and inability to perform at expected levels, and they fear that liberated energy will lead to humiliation again. To prevent this they will implode—hold themselves in—and they will be cautious interpersonally. They will invite others to come closer, but as intimacy develops the fear of invasion and loss of autonomy increases, and they will create barriers to greater closeness through indirect maneuvering. These individuals have been invaded, and they believe closeness will lead to further invasion. They can't imagine that autonomy and intimacy, freedom and connection, can coexist, so they bounce erratically between coming forward and backing up. In no other psychological difficulty is it more important that splits be resolved. Almost every part of us can be integrated, or at least partially resolved, if self-knowledge and dialogue become an ongoing process in living.

THE ISSUE OF CREATIVITY AND DIRECTION

It has been said that you cannot say "yes" unless you have—truly have—the capacity to support and express your "no." If one lacks the ability to negate or refuse, a yes becomes simply acquiescing, passive drifting, accommodation, or conforming, and, as such, is not a reflection of a person's deeper self. The ability to say "no" is a statement of our autonomy, our separateness. Next comes the deeper ability to initiate, to say "yes" based on internal excitement, aliveness, and desire. "Yes, I'll go out with you. Yes, I'll be your friend. Yes, I want to make love to you. Yes, I'll get the job done." All are statements that are deepened by true choice, by the ability and willingness to say no or yes.

On the other hand a person who can't say yes has a weakened no. If we can only negate, we cease to experience choice as well. We are continually opting for limits, safety, sameness and regression, and the habitual no becomes an unconscious lifestyle with little sense of the process of decision. Recognizing that one is creating a life through the yes and no process, and accepting that responsibility, is a part of experiencing the tremendous strength and potency that is ours as consciously evolved beings on the earth.

In the last section we discussed how important negation was in terms of self-definition. "I'm not that," is the first step in our developing self-consciousness, and often is an initial step in self-definition throughout our lives. And yet if I'm not that, what am I? Saying no is always a response, and, as such, it places one in the position of respondent—a valid, but limited, stance. To go beyond the negation, one must allow for *initiation*, and this is a process of not only knowing what one is not, but what one *is*—not only knowing what one is against, but what one is for. Initiation requires more self-knowledge—more maturity. When we are initiating, we are coming into the world from an internal impulse, an emerging urge, a self-expression that (when expressed) is more personally revealing than a respondent reaction. Verbally we come from initiating positions by beginning our sentences with the word "I." I want. I prefer. I think. I feel. I see this in that. I stand here. I created this. I value that. I am moved by you.

Play with the words yes and no and you will likely discover a felt difference between the two. Not always predictable, "no" often has the pleasureable sensation of closing, protecting, hardening and creating safety. "Yes" often has the pleasure of softening, opening, excitement and forwardness. I use the word "pleasure" in both cases, assuming that the yes or no is conscious, resolved and supported. To the degree that one or more of these conditions are not present, pleasure will be diminished.

The respondent position is, of course, one of yes or no. As a respondent, I have less control and must wait for my stimulus. I am faced with impotency, but I am spared possible rejection and the vulnerability of possible ridicule or rejected initiation. As an initiator, I don't have to wait, so the power and control is mine. I am the boy choosing when to cross the high school gymnasium to initiate contact with the selected girl among her peers. But I am also the exposing one, the one who shows his preference, his heart, his desire. Both responder and initiator have special pleasure and potential pain. Life is composed of one's unique relationship to both as illustrated in the following therapy fantasy.

In discussing her tendency to come from a respondent position, Sharon described how frightened she often was. It was as if she were in a game of dodgeball, waiting to get smashed.

I asked her to imagine such a predicament and she did. In her fantasy she was the only one in the middle of the circle. On the perimeter of the circle were the people of her life, and as she was free to move she began to enjoy her star status. She was good at dodging and it was fun; she realized she didn't have to be anyone's stationary target. This, in and of itself, was useful to her, as she came in touch with how she stayed stuck in interaction with people whose primary desire was to use or abuse her.

Extending the fantasy further, I asked her how she might reorganize it so that she was no longer the target. She quickly exclaimed, "Oh, that's easy. I'll give myself the ball." In doing this she became the initiator, and had the excitement of being the star from the opposite position, tagging others at will with her accurate arm.

Initiation can be a very high level of living—a form of behavior that can lend itself to high energy and intense feeling—and, as such, it needs a great deal of internal and/or external support. In the above example Sharon, as the respondent, needed only to be quick and responsive. But when she got the ball she had to make her choice of target, decide how to approach it, decide how hard to throw, and decide what to do if she missed.

We will involve ourselves in the experimental, expansive, aggressive mode of the yes if we have enough internal strength, a safe enough environment, and the right to return to our no whenever necessary. In the earlier case example, if Anita had had a firm comfort with her no, she could have allowed me more space to suggest experiments, because she could say no at any point. With even greater comfort and self-support, she could initiate experiments both inside and outside of therapy as she moves forward in creating a richer outer and inner life.

Thus far we have discussed initiation primarily on an interpersonal level. Freud saw it interpersonally as he described this developmental stage as involving the resolution of the Oedipal conflict. In such a resolution a child feels the desire to move toward the parent of the opposite sex, establishing a prototype for later male-female relating. This is a process in which male or female five-year-olds have their first "crush." It is their first self-initiating movement toward a heartfelt, desired object after the individuation process of establishing autonomy. But Freud also reminded us that the two primary capacities established in a healthy individual are the abilities to love and work, and the latter is the second emphasis for initiative.

To know in a heartfelt way what one loves to do, what activities stir us the most, is the basis for a deep, initiating thrust and direction. Just as we have a sense of who we want to move toward, so we can have a sense of what excites us in the way of human endeavor. This sense is made known to us through our natural curiosity, interest, desire, excitement and love. We love that which, and those who, stir and support our inner sense of pleasure, and this pleasure fosters our willingness to commit. Out of this commitment comes our attention and thought, our exploration, destructuring and restructuring—which is often referred to as the creative movement.

By creative movement I am referring to the process of organizing internal and external elements into meaningful wholes. It can be seen on a broad scale when we describe how we create a life-style. Or on a more "here and now" basis as we come in touch with our unfolding life from moment to moment. The amount of our life's creativity or originality

has a direct correlation with three underpinnings. The first is
the degree to which we have access to our own inner stirrings,
primarily our feeling and intuitive sense. The second has to
do with how clearly we see what is available in the environment in terms of raw materials, talent, potential and resources. The third rests on how much freedom, support and
focus we have to bring the two together.

If an individual's first initiating movements towards
people or creative endeavor are routinely rejected, he/she
may well close off to deep wanting and desire. They will
avoid knowing what is closest to their hearts because this
kind of experience has led them to disapproval. Imagine a
five-year-old as their love or excitement stirs for someone or
something within their reach. Imagine their wide open joy in
reaching out for the object of their desire. Imagine someone criticizing or rejecting this movement. Crestfallenness
(falling from the crest of excitement) is the result. Consistent
rejection is eventually internalized against the wants and
reaching, until gradually the acknowledgment of wanting and
the urge to reach is extinguished.

When one is cut off from the heart, a major source of
aliveness and direction ceases to exist. Where will one turn
for these? Production and control often become substitutes
for aliveness. We become less focused on feeling and more
interested in achievement. We become compulsive achiev-
ers, controlling ourselves (to avoid our deepest wants), and
attempting to control our environment through excessive
ordering, maneuvering and performing. Since we are out of
touch with our desire, we invest much of our life energy in
our pride. We create an image of ourselves, and spend much
of our life energy maintaining the picture we have created.
We have no wants or needs. We do not reach out to others.
We allow connection only through their need for us.

In this stance we rely on rules of conduct for our direction. Our favorite words and concepts include appropriateness,

independence, strength, power, superiority, winning, will power, and competence.

> Bob mentioned during one of our sessions that, for him, life had always been a race. In overt and covert ways he was constantly attempting to stay "out in front." I asked him to imagine himself in a race. As he did so, he began to feel the exhilaration of winning, of being in first place. Asking him to continue the fantasy, he went on in great detail, describing his effort, his watching over his shoulder, his feeling of smugness, and his sense of thrill. As the fantasy wore on, he became aware of his will power, a kind of mind over matter stance, which began to have a vague anxiety to it. He also began to be aware of some dissatisfaction with being alone. To maintain superiority as a constant lifestyle, one must forego being a part of the pack, literally joining the human "race."

Bob's budding anxiousness and loneliness are positive signs in the process of returning to underlying wants and needs. His anxiety points to his fear of humanness, which he abandoned years ago when he was rejected and threatened. His loneliness is the price he pays for a hostile competitive stance, one which flies the banner of, "I'm nothing unless I'm ahead."

Lest I be misunderstood, let me make it clear that I am in no way minimizing accomplishment as an enlivening human experience. Alfred Adler (1927) wrote how mastery was a primary motivator and source of pleasure for mankind, and I agree. But it is extremely important to ascertain the intent of the achievement. If it is to maintain superiority, it is in the service of the ego. To maintain an ego image is interpersonally, and intrapersonally, divisive. Interpersonally, it cuts one off from others (out in front in the race). Intrapersonally, it cuts one off from one's deeper feelings. Heartfelt achievement is not in comparison to others, but is in search of one's excellence. It is interested in excellence in oneself *and* others. It's not you or me, but you *and* me, and life's race becomes one of each helping the other to reach their potential. Love becomes an important stance in this orientation, and it is to a love of people, endeavor and life, that our prideful, independent friend Bob must return.

This closes our chapter on core character development. We have discussed how we organize around the major existential issues of existence, need, separateness, feeling and direction. These issues are resolved in a prototypical way during the first six years of life. Each of us will have work to do with each of these issues, depending on conditions along each step in our historical and developmental path. We will have major work to do where our caretakers had strong unresolved issues of their own and were unable to help us because of their deficit. Life goes on beyond six, however, and we return to these issues over and over again, to feel our stuckness, or to rework the issues in a way which helps us to reorganize them.

We also deal increasingly with a larger world, a world which confronts us with the old lessons and provides us with some new ones. We begin to form our identity in some interpersonal ways beyond and including the intrapersonal dynamic issues described heretofore. The thrust of life is toward an ever expanded internal and external world, and it is to this expansion that we will now turn.

4

The Interpersonal Aspects of
Self-Diminishment

Thus far we have discussed our development and self-loss in terms of intrapersonal issues, but as we grow there are interactional forces that come to play on our identity. Alfred Adler, a social psychology theorist, emphasized the importance of social connectedness as a motivator for human behavior. In using this framework much of what we do has the impetus of establishing our significance within our social group. Thus behavior is less caused as it is goal oriented. In using this model, we look less to the past for behavioral roots than to the future for the behavior's intent, that is, what we are trying to accomplish in the behavior we exhibit.

If establishing a place for ourselves within a social milieu is a primary need for human beings (and I believe it is), then we can reflect readily on how each of us developed personality characteristics to mesh with and fit into our family of origin. We can also extend this to look at our current group memberships to determine what patterns continue or recur. As with any self-exploration model, structure, group roles, patterns, and characteristics can help us get a deeper sense of this elusive phenomenon called identity, and simultaneously give us a view of unnecessary self-limits.

To start the exploration of ourselves as community members, we must begin with the family, our first community. There are generalizations about birth order and family constellation that can be a useful starting point for individual reflection. By birth order I am referring to where one fits chronologically in one's family of origin. Such a random event has powerful character-shaping influence on many of us. As we begin this section on family constellation, it might be useful to the reader to muse on his own first group experience. What was your unique place? How did you establish and maintain your specialness in your original group, your family of origin?

THE ONLY CHILD

Only children have a special place by being the *only* child. This can also be true for only girls in a family of boys or vice versa. Specialness can be negative or positive, but when someone is the only one of anything, he or she has a definite impact because of their difference.

Only children have the advantage of often being important, an experience which can lend itself to a solid sense of worthiness. They often have a concomitant attitude of having a right to the good things in life. They may have been indulged with attention, material goods, praise, love and comfort, and because they are used to this from others, they may have developed attitudes which continue to illicit such responses throughout their life. Comfort with indulgence, truly allowing it to be experienced, is a blessing.

There are three major drawbacks that can come out of being an only child. Ironically, the first has to do with being important. Importance can be a blessing and it can be a heavy burden. If one is extraordinarily special, he will often carry the responsibility of proving he is worthy of such an exalted position. Parental demands can easily become self demands and pressures which can last a lifetime. The injunction not to disappoint Mom and Dad can be transferred to the world in later years, to include never disappointing anyone—a tremendous weight. These demands often require that a child grow up quickly to join adult parents in adult ways of being. The description of some children being "four going on forty" is reflective of such a telescoped maturational process. Such maturation and high self-expectation, however, does not allow for many childhood experiences or a time-cured foundation for adult responsibilities. Such early maturity often rests on a brittle foundation.

Being the "different one" in a family setting can also result in having the same kind of identity as a core sense of oneself. "I'm different," can be self-enhancing and is true for all of us, but it can also be destructively separating. Not being raised with other children, one can miss the relieving, freeing experience of being just one of the kids, just part of the world of children.

Finally, exclusive attention in early life sets up a cycle of interpersonal caring that can be limiting.

Mary was describing the interaction between her friend Steve, his seven-year-old daughter and herself on a Saturday afternoon. In this interaction she had felt anxious and jealous as Steve seemed to be caught up in what his daughter was doing and saying. This wasn't an issue of his not attending to her enough, as she was satisfied with his attentiveness in general. It was, as she became clearer, an issue of her having a limited capacity to feel loved and cared about unless she was the center of attention.

Being the center of attention is one way of being loved, and for the only child it can be the most common; but because life affords only one center stage infrequently it is not enough. Mary's pattern had been to feel anxious or demand more attention when someone else was attended to for any length of time. An alternative was to open up to the possibility of feeling loved or at peace while on the periphery.

To do this one has to develop the art of being nourished through observation, through being a non-participating audience. It requires a letting go of self-focus which can be frightening. Many of us resist allowing our interest and curiosity to flower, and to let ourselves delight in the simple presence of others, trusting that we will be O.K. and that our time for center stage will naturally come again.

The Oldest Child

Oldest children share in some of the trends of only children. They are likely to grow up fast, have a highly developed sense of responsibility, and are strongly self-controlled and controlling of others.

One can readily see the reliability and strength that comes from such characteristics. Oldest children are often the leaders and "doers" of our society. In their family of origin, particularly if they are female, they find their place by becoming little adults, particularly when parents are unavailable through death, employment or emotional limits. Oldest children will serve as secondary parents for their younger brothers and sisters. This adult role may include bossiness, protectiveness, compulsiveness and excessive organization as they attempt to take on tasks that are beyond their natural abilities.

Taking on a parenting role when one is so young results in major losses. Oldest children often become the protectors when they actually need protection. They need guidance and discipline, yet they must find a way to supply this for others. They need love and nourishment yet must often settle for respect as others marvel at "how grown up you are." They will often rise to the occasion, but the upward stance will lack the depth that comes from natural evolution. To support the responsibilities that they assume, they will often turn to a rigid stance, one that relies on rules, a black and white orientation. Such a position does offer direction, but ignores their humanness and the humanness of others in their lives. Without this, life becomes somewhat mechanical.

To become less mechanical, one must let go of the rising-above stance that was necessary, but unfair and untimely years before. What has been lost are the characteristics of childhood: playfulness, silliness, wonderment, craziness, vulnerability, spontaneity, looseness, and laughter. A friend of mine who is married to a first daughter says he loves it when his wife has a belly laugh. He cherishes these moments, I believe, because he loves her and knows, at some level, how she's been cheated, and cheats herself of the aliveness of letting go and falling (from the rational, rule oriented, productive orientation). If one can allow letting go, one can begin to fall in many ways. One can fall in love, fall apart, fall down on the job, or fall into someone's arms. One'll come back up again, but in a more natural, inner directed manner.

THE YOUNGEST CHILD

Picture for a moment the youngest sibling. What comes to mind? Likely you will envision a child tagging along, begrudgingly included, trying to catch up. You might also see a child who interacts from a place of inadequacy and inequality. Youngest children don't have the skills or resources of their older brothers and sisters, and are often in the position of being helped, served or taught.

Internalized, this position in the family can become an identity of "I'm not enough. I'm not good enough. I'm not big enough. I don't count." Youngest children often have not been taken seriously, and as a result they don't take themselves seriously. Or they constantly fight to make an impact. Finally, there may be a strong impetus in the youngest to improve or to catch up, which might be phrased, "I'm not good enough now, but I will be when I. . ." If this is a strong theme, it can become a life-pervasive force in that we will never catch up. There will always be another mountain to climb, and someone will always be one step ahead.

> John was aware of using too many words when speaking with others, and yet the compulsion to talk, repeat his points and keep the floor was strong. The result was that people often tuned him out, often before they were truly bored, as they anticipated being in for a long monologue.
>
> I asked John to fill the room with words, and he began to ramble. As he did so, sadness began to well up in him, a sadness that, with focus, began to elicit memories of his days as the youngest child in a family of four.
>
> He remembered the glazed look of family members as he began to speak, a look which excluded him from full family membership. He remembered also making repeated attempts to get through to them with words, to little avail.

When I asked him how else he might get through, John smiled as he imagined simply saying, "I see I'm not getting through to you," or emphasizing to his conversation partner, "This is important, give me your attention."

Not counting, not feeling good enough, in the youngest child or in any of us, can set the stage for many other self-defeating behaviors. If I imagine I can't do a task, I am likely to insist that you take over. This demonstration of demanding may be heightened if you refuse, or if I begin to feel more fear around competency issues. It is a demand that comes out of a fear of my (real or imagined) inadequacy or of being left behind. Taken to the extreme, such demanding requires that our intimate others remain in our service constantly.

Support, help, instruction and protection are all wonderful experiences that are familiar to our youngest family member. When our need for them dominates, however, they may block the high energy associated with the opposite stance of being a protector, a teacher, a helper and a leader. Going it alone allows us the thrill of independence and mastery. Being a resource to another affords us the softer glow that comes through contribution and interdependency.

THE MIDDLE CHILD

The child who begins life in the middle may establish that position throughout life. A middle child can often see and appreciate differing positions since he/she has had experience in viewing older and younger siblings as they establish opposite and sometimes opposing behaviors.

Being able to see and appreciate difference is a desirable trait, particularly in its support of loving relationships. It can, however, lend itself to ambivalence, ambiguity and confusion in terms of being grounded in a firm position. If both positions are valid, where do I stand? What do I believe? What is my preference? For whom will I vote?

As I am a middle child, I have particular appreciation for the benefits and costs that often accompany this family constellation position. It is no doubt an important factor in my choice of profession, as it is easy for me to see how multi-colored life is, as opposed to the black-and-white attitudes that others favor. It is easy for me to understand and make room for my clients without excessive judgment. There is no right way for any of us to live, simply a way that works toward our fulfillment or against it.

The cost of my middle-of-the-road stance has been alluded to previously. It became particularly apparent to me a decade ago when I had the following experience:

My family—my father, stepmother, older sister, younger brother and I—had gotten together for a holiday meal. During the conversation at the dinner table an argument began, and grew more heated by the moment.

My brother and sister expressed old resentments toward all family members, some of the anger being an attempt to complete old, unfinished business. As the anger intensified, I moved into an arbitrator position, facilitating communication, defusing anger when it grew too hot, and bringing dialogue to some resolution. My family appreciated this contribution from me, as I helped them limit the degree of destructive potential in such a confrontation.

The price I paid for such a stance occurred to me as I rode home that evening. I had avoided my own anger, my own unfinished business with each of them. By helping them get clear as to their stance, I had avoided taking one of my own. By softening the interaction I had refused to allow change to come out of harsh confrontation, and I had used the role of intellectual observer to stay personally hidden.

Weeks later my sister told me that my brother had complained about my being so understanding. He had wished aloud that I would sometimes "just get angry and tell him so."

Taken to the extreme, the arbitrator role leaves one a non-entity without feelings, needs, irrationality and human-ness. Such an individual will have difficulty finding a true place in the world. This doesn't mean that the arbitrator is not useful or appreciated. It means, rather, that one will be seen more in terms of one's skill, talent and utility, and less in terms of one's deeper essence. In order to truly belong, in order to truly have a place, we must be seen. This includes our talents, but cannot be limited to them.

I have used the family constellation as a vehicle for exploring our development in the context of social interaction. Thus far we have emphasized the impact of the family, but the broader world awaited each of us, a world that would influence us as we learned to influence it. It is to that world that we now turn.

FROM FAMILY TO SCHOOL

Take a moment to remember your first day of leaving home for school. It is a prototypic scene that will be repeated throughout life, that of leaving the familiar to expand into the foreign. It can be, and often is, an exciting or anxiety-filled time, depending on the amount of support available. For the grammar school child it is the first peer-oriented testing ground for his newly developed character. Trust, autonomy and initiative come to the fore once again for us in kindergarten or in subsequent situations that present the unfamiliar. Can I trust the benevolence of these strangers? Will they provide what I need? If not, will I be able to protect myself, and aggressively create positive interaction? Will they respect my limits, my privacy, my space? If not, will I be able to stand firm against opposition? And finally, will others make room for my initiative, creative impulses, and expression, and will I allow them to emerge and be shared?

In addition to reworking old issues within a broader context, there are new issues for the latency age child. They include containment, the beginning of group consciousness and performance mastery.

Containment is the ability to hold an impulse, to allow one's outflow of movement to pause, expand and develop. Its beginnings are in the home, but serious containment comes about in the presence of peers in the classroom setting. The fairness aspect of containment is often emphasized at school in the form of taking turns, but containment is more than this at its highest level. It is first of all a way to allow feeling time to deepen and expand. This is not to discount impulsivity and spontaneity, but to value a process where feeling is not habitually spilled before it has a chance to fill us up completely. Secondly, containment can allow us to develop our receptive facility. Containment in this manner is not simply a way of being courteous or polite, but becomes an ability which allows us nourishment through receiving the thoughts, feelings, perceptions and essence of another.

Containment can develop best in a non-competitive atmosphere where one sees peers as contributors rather than opponents. It is as true in adulthood as in childhood, that we truly dialogue with those whom we trust—trusting that our time will come, that this conversation is not a race, and that our value as human beings is not being critiqued. Dialogues at best have a sharing, exploring flavor as opposed to a personal comparing, competitive one. This is not to suggest that dialogues will always, or even often, be egalitarian. Someone will often be more knowledgeable, more talented or articulate in a group interchange. It simply means that differences are not used to determine overall human value. There is no hidden agenda behind the exchange.

This author holds a similar philosophy regarding the development of performance mastery. Early schooling is an age when we are surrounded by new opportunities in intellectual development, musical performace, art, athletics, tool use, dance and social contact. I use the word "opportunity" consciously here, as that is ideally what our schooling should afford. The school experience, however, is often a competitive one, a system which can often subtly, and not so subtly, influence us to turn our backs on experiences in which we don't excel.

Many adults have blocks to participating in certain endeavors—blocks which originated in early school experiences. Friends of mine are reluctant to participate in athletics because of their early lack of gracefulness and the response it brought. They were the last ones chosen for team sports, and to this day associate physical activity with humiliation. My wife is hesitant about musical involvement, stemming at least partially from her exclusion from the school choir because of her "substandard" voice. I have had to work with a tendency to catastrophize around using tools, and remember my embarassment and dissappointment when I was banned from the kindergarten tool room because I had cut myself with a saw.

These first associations and impressions about who we are in relation to activities are powerful in self-definition and self-limitation. There are two primary premises on which activity exclusion rests. They are both judgments and as such are learned from our surroundings. The first judgment is that only those with a natural bent or talent for a pursuit should pursue it. When I took up the violin five years ago, a friend of mine reflected this point of view when he exclaimed, "Oh,—I didn't know you had any musical talent." We need not be talented or strive for excellence as a ticket of admission to involvement. There is joy inherent in the process of most endeavors, and additional joy in fluidness as we engage in them. If we then develop talent and excellence, it is icing on the cake. We miss a lot of the sweetness of living though, when we don't join in because, "I'm not very good at that," or "I don't think I have much potential."

The second premise that discourages life participation is that "life is a contest to be won." Related to the premise that we should only be involved if we have talent, this premise states that we will only include ourselves, or be included by others, if we have a chance to be the best. Winning adds the experience of triumphing over others, and our school systems rest on such principles. They reflect our society's competitive emphasis.

It is not my intent here to devalue the system or argue its merits, but simply to point out what we lose with the emphasis described above. Any of us who have enjoyed an excellent musical performance, have thrilled to an athlete's grace, or felt awed by a scientist's discovery, have been responding to the achievement of excellence. Our fellow human beings can add excitement to our lives as they come close to the edge of what is possible. My point is that if we only thrill to *their* achievement then we miss something vital in terms of first-hand experience. We miss our own music making, our own gracefulness and our own experience of study and discovery. It matters little that someone else can do it better. It is more important that we not miss the process of *our* living.

ADOLESCENCE, THE BRIDGE TO ADULTHOOD

Latency age years (6-12) hopefully give us many opportunities for belonging, varied experience and mastery—raw material out of which a sense of self can begin to form. It is during the teen years that we integrate many of our life experiences into some kind of self-concept, some cohesive sense of identity. This sense of self has, of course, been developing all along, but it is during our adolescence that it is tested and altered within a context of greater freedom and independence. This is also a time when this sense of self begins to form our future, as we choose education and career paths. These directions come out of self-perception, interest, and values—all essential elements in self-concept.

It is not only a time of pulling together the past and choosing paths into the future, however. There are bedrock issues at this point in life around emerging maleness and femaleness. Developing sexuality, physical stature and relationships with the opposite sex pose intense issues for self-concept resolution—issues which, if not comfortably resolved, pose major impediments to free flowing energy and aliveness in later life.

Richard had been raised in a family which had a strong repressive attitude toward sensuality and sexuality. His father related to the world primarily through power over others. With Richard he had been excessively oppressive around most impulses, so that his son felt fear in relation to his father.

As we worked together in a therapy session, Richard recalled a time when he was fifteen. His older sister's friend had come home with her from college. Richard had been working out with weights for some time and was feeling pretty proud of his body, so he walked into the kitchen bare from the waist up, an exhibition primarily aimed at impressing his sister's friend. His father's response was cutting (castrating) as he admonished his son to stop showing off and go put a shirt on, an exposing response which humiliated Richard as he slid out of the room.

His father's attitude toward his son's budding maleness had stayed with Richard well into his thirties. He still had difficulty feeling his maleness and showing it to women. Our work in my office literally began with his focusing on and feeling his pelvis. Once he could center himself there, we began experimenting with walking, talking and responding with this new groundedness. Quite literally, his work consisted of learning to come from the lower half of his body.

It is essential for men and women to learn to be comfortable with and support their masculinity and femininity. It is the center of our aliveness. When I encouraged Richard to come from his pelvis, I wasn't encouraging him to create a macho image. Someone who is macho is compensating for a lack of sexual connection—living in an image. But a man or woman who feels their male or female energy is full of themselves, enjoys their gender and the opposite sex, and loves the interaction of male/female interplay. Richard needed to regain his pride; he needed to strut and show off. In essence, the way back to himself in this work was for him to become the interrupted teenager in the kitchen so that he could complete this gestalt.

As teenagers wrestle with the issue of identity, they are bombarded with first experiences. First dates, first jobs, first cars, first loves, first sex, first . . . the list goes on and on.

They are becoming a man or woman over time, and the independence underlying such a transformation yields a host of prototypic experiences which leave strong impressions which will create character and will form lives. This is the push of history that we have described in this book as a motivator of human behavior. To understand one's behavior, one must understand one's personal history. It is also important to understand one's direction and goals. What motivations and values elicit certain behaviors? What is one trying to accomplish in life? All behavior springs from the meaning one gives life and has its rudimentary inception during adolescent identity formulation.

Each of us is guided by our values, although our stated values may be quite different from our true guiding principles. Values are the basis on which we make commitments, and it is the ability to make and keep commitments which distinguishes the adult from the child. In my work with clients, discovering values is an important task, as often one's life and most cherished values are out of sync. Although we are guided by many values and our values may change at different ages, we can often find a primary philosophy from which much of our living is based. For some this guiding principle is to earn a future reward. For some security and safety is most important. For others personal perfection serves as a structure for activity. Still others seek maximum acquisition.

This book is based on my personal value of cultivating awareness and a deepening experience of self toward greater aliveness. If I am congruent, I will organize my living toward that end or remind myself of these values when my living patterns conflict significantly with my stated goals. On the other hand, if we consistently live in opposition to our goals, it may well be that our true value system eludes us.

Thus far, this book has focused on what we may have lost during our journey in life. We have discussed the love and pleasure of the infant, the autonomy of the toddler, the creativity and imagination of the preschooler and the industry, playfulness and fun of the pre-teenager. We have touched on the romance and adventure of the adolescent, and in the rest of the book we will address the reality and responsibility of the adult. (These are Alexander Lowen's categories, *Bioenergetics*, p.60.)

These major areas of possible loss, and the other ones mentioned in previous chapters, are simply starting places for most of us, as we examine our daily lives and our blocks to full living. Because we began life with unique constitutions and had unique histories, each of us will discover unique rhythms and patterns as we live out our lives. Our differences will become more apparent the deeper we explore. The more we attend to ourselves the better we will become at recognizing our energy in its gross and subtle changes, and at creating our lives out of this awareness.

SECTION II

THE CONSEQUENCES OF LOSS

5

Depression and Anxiety

Depression and anxiety are two of the most common symptoms of the self-loss we have been discussing. Although most of us experience both depression and anxiety, it is likely that we will be more prone to one or the other when we get off balance. They both represent energetic disorders within the body.

Depression is often characterized by despondency and low energy, which is manifested in a low activity level, and an apathetic attitude toward life. It may also be accompanied by critical self-judgment or self-hate. There is almost always a sense of despair or pessimism about the future and often there are self-recriminations about the past.

The word "depression," in and of itself, offers a description of the dynamic process involved in such a symptom. The depressed person is depressing something, some form of energy. Perhaps anger. Therefore, when we meet a depressed man or woman, we might suspect that we are encountering an angry person who is out of touch with, or has little support for, their anger. Anger may be just the beginning, and often is. Sadness and fear are often depressed as well as joy and sexuality. When one is depressed, all energy forms are likely to be reduced or absent. Anger and resentment are often the first to be encountered in self-exploration, however, as they serve as a dam to spontaneous, flowing vitality.

> Paul offers a fairly common scenario for situational depression when he came into therapy on the heels of a divorce. He was depressed. During sessions he would get in touch with a great deal of anger directed toward himself for "blowing it." This kind of self-blaming anger was not useful to alleviate his depression, as he would simply get tighter in his body, driving the "blamed" part of him even deeper into a hole. His life had become a cycle of either experiencing the blamer in an energetic, wailing harangue, or the accused in a depressed, burdened silence.
>
> What was missing for Paul and many others in his situation was a willingness to express the secret anger he held toward his wife (and originally his mother) for leaving him. She had initiated the separation and continued to refuse a reconciliation. I'm in no way indicating that she was the culprit, but that he was disowning the part of him that was calling her just that.

Alexander Lowen gives us a character description of individuals who are likely to experience depression in his book, *Depression and the Body* (1972). In it he describes the depressed person as a waiter. They wait for what they want, and because of this quality they are dependent on the benevolence of the world around them. They are victims through inaction. They don't aggress. When they are actively depressed they don't have the energy to move out to the world—so they are passive. When they are more charged up internally, they still lack the internal permission to create a life that is nourishing—so they return to a waiting stance.

Aggression requires energy and produces energy. The depressed person either doesn't have energy or can't use the energy they have to create more.

The depressed person is also one who has given up childhood early in order to please a parent who was uncomfortable with dependency and youthfulness. When a child does this to please a parent, however, he leaves behind much of his liveliness and juice. He abandons his innocence, spontaneity, imagination, lightness and fun. No wonder a depressed person is angry. He has given up much of the energy that makes life a dance.

To compensate for the energetic loss described above, one will often turn to will power and mechanical rules for support and direction. Unable to create life out of one's heart one will turn to their head.

One of the ironies of such a compensation is that someone who has sacrificed their childhood and continues to repress the natural child within, does so, at least partially, to elicit connection and love—initially from unloving parents and later from family and friends in their adult lives. The irony is this—we are loved to a large degree for the aliveness we exhibit—for who we are. The depressed person was asked very early to give up his essence, and now has an illusion that if he is ever loved, it will come from what he does or produces. He has given up the essence out of which love from others could come.

Each of these aspects of depression—repression, waiting, premature abandonment of childhood, and an excessive orientaton to will power and productivity—suggests an avenue toward health. A depressed person needs to express rather than depress. When he finds himself to be a victim, he must recognize his choice and find a way to initiate action. He must encourage a re-emergence of the child within, offering it the kind of support that was absent the first time around, and he must use will power more judiciously, replacing it more often with desire and self-expression.

ANXIETY

Anxiety is experienced as a vague dread or apprehension. It is an unformed feeling, a feeling which may remain unformed because we fear it. It can also be simply our unwillingness to feel fear itself in a more direct way. No matter what feeling is being kept out of consciousness, however, the basis for anxiety is a lack of support—a lack of internal or external support for an emerging gestalt.

Margaret often started our sessions with a report of feeling anxious. Staying with the sensation helped somewhat in reducing her discomfort, but the basic feeling remained. In one session, although she reported anxiety, she looked excited. Focusing on that word, and saying, "I'm excited," changed the sensation more toward one of pleasure.

Using a tried and true bioenergetic edict that anxiety is excitement without breath, I asked her to express the phrase "I'm excited," as she expanded her breath in her chest and belly. The sensation became even more enjoyable with breath support.

In later sessions as she felt even more self-support, she was able to add the interpersonal element to the feeling. The expression became, "I'm excited to see you." At one time in her life she had lost the support for her natural excitement, and when it emerged she diffused it. Anxiety was the result. Now she was finding increasing support for natural feeling.

Identifying the emerging gestalt, finding a way to support it (internally or externally), expressing it and taking action in relation to it, are all ways to reduce anxiety and convert it into feelings which can allow for completion.

We cannot always be supported, of course, but there is an optimal level of support for all of us during each phase in our lives. We know if we are within range by our sense of ourselves in our body. If we are overly supported for too long, we begin to atrophy. Too far out beyond our support, and we become anxious. Some of us are prone to stay too far back from our growing edge. Others leave their ground in a wild, overly stimulating life of avoiding experience by excessive activity.

We do not make ourselves anxious by life participation alone, however. Far from it. Some of us overcharge ourselves with our thoughts. We go into the future, stimulating our bodies with "home movies." For various reasons we are catastrophizing the future—in rehearsing it we are concerned about whether we will get applause or tomatoes for our behavior. Will we be able to control outcomes? Will life add up to the pictures we create and hold so dear?

Others create anxiety by pretending—pretending they are still helpless children—pretending they can't be loved for who they are—pretending they are not human beings similar to everyone else. When we come close to changing one of those pretends, or making any other change, our anxiety may increase even more, as we may feel unsupported in a new way of being. This is part of the reason why real personal change is slow. It's a dance of change—finding support, changing some more, and so on.

Whether anxiety comes from an internal conflict, futurizing or pretends, or all three, reducing anxiety progresses when one can become grounded. Grounding means support. Bioenergetically, it means the support one feels by being in one's body and feeling the earth below. It literally means

"being on solid ground." Bioenergetically, it also means having
the support of one's breath which keeps one's metabolic fires
burning at the level needed for the task at hand. Finally, in a
bioenergetic sense it means having the optimal amount of
tension within your body to accommodate the moment.

But support comes from many other areas. It comes
from a sense of one's history, as in the recent "Roots"
interest, and it comes at least partially from knowing where
you're going. It comes from what you put in your body as
well as what you do with it. It comes interpersonally through
friends that hold you up when you're depleted or profes-
sionals that assist when you break down.

Most importantly, support is garnered by one's ability to
be in the now, to stay with one's present process. Just as
anxiety destroys awareness with its cloaking vagueness,
focused awareness destroys anxiety. "Here I am, my butt's
on the chair, I'm in my body and I'm using my senses to
orient myself to what is. From there I'll use my resources to
respond."

Finally, groundedness can be achieved and anxiety al-
layed by consciously allowing oneself to back up, to consciously choose regression.

> John commented at the beginning of our session that he
> felt anxious, and that he could sense a barrier between us. I
> asked him to maintain and reinforce that barrier, experi-
> encing himself behind it. He did so and began to feel
> increased comfort as he acknowledged his surrounding wall.
> As the experiment continued, he began to experience the
> wall as "thinning out" until, toward the end of the session, it
> had become transparent and he felt in better contact with
> me.

We are all human beings who, if supported adequately, will choose growth over stagnation. We need to regress and withdraw, however, to replenish and protect ourselves regularly. If we can allow ourselves this kind of safety, the courage to move forward will emerge in good time.

6

Maintaining Self-Loss

In my view few of us are living as fully as we might. We have learned to distrust our feelings and ignore our rhythms. On both a community and individual level, we value power over feeling and doing over being (accomplishment over process). As a result we seldom plumb the depths of our experience, and can't be available for another's. The symptoms of such an orientation on an individual level are the ubiquitous complaints of anxiety, depression, boredom and emptiness. Interpersonally and nationally, this loss of self lends itself to superficiality, impotence, irresolvable conflict, deadness, withdrawal and boredom. A significant number of us are recognizing our symptoms as reflective of values that miss the mark, or a focus that is too exclusive or limiting. This kind of recognition contains seeds from which self-exploration and recovery may blossom.

The beginning direction and focus for such a journey is inward toward greater familiarization with one's physical experience, feeling, and intellectual organization (beliefs, rules, etc.). Even with the hope of greater vitality and aliveness, it is a path strewn with personal reluctance and resistance. Wanting to know and defending against knowing is a dance that goes on in all of us in and out of therapy, and is often the initial focus in therapy. As we increase our awareness of our resistance and our desire to know more, we expand our self-experience and begin making way for new possibilities.

THE SELF'S REPLACEMENT

Nature abhors a vacuum. If there is an empty space, something will fill it. So when we tuned ourselves out in an attempt to accommodate our early environment, we needed to fill the resultant empty space with something—something to hold on to. Something to give us direction. Something to give us a sense of substance. Something to share with the world. This something was and is based on thoughts and words—descriptions that we create as to how things are and how we are. They are self-substitutes when we lack the support for authenticity and good contact with our surroundings.

Another word for this self-substitute is "image." We create an image largely because we don't experience or trust ourselves and our ever-changing process. We become the intellectual, the sufferer, the rebel, the giver, the challenger, or the enlightened being. We may sustain an image by developing it as a profession and overidentifying ourselves as teachers, psychologists, businessmen and women, doctors, missionaries or policemen.

With each of these images we assume a stance, a way of being that is not, in and of itself, detrimental. As a police-man, I take a stance of policing, of maintaining order. As a teacher I orient to providing thoughts and stimulating others to think. As I suffer, I am in touch with an important aspect of living which comes out of my own and the world's imperfection. All of these ways of being are potentially enlivening when they come out of natural process. They are deadening to the degree that we become hardened and cannot allow room for another gestalt to arise.

> Sharon was a tragedy queen. She was a therapist who, if she didn't have a current tragedy of her own, would always have a sad story to tell about a client or friend. It was her way of making contact, and it worked to some degree, as tragedy has a way of interesting most of us.
>
> The difficulty for Sharon, however, was that she didn't trust other parts of herself to come forward for long. She had the belief that she was basically uninteresting, so she had her "story" ready whenever she suspected others were about to turn away.
>
> Ironically, as is often the case, her attempt to keep other's attention through tragedy was exactly what led to their becoming disinterested. One cannot thrive on, or stay interested in, tragedy alone. So relationships with Sharon became short lived or were limited to those who would stay with the drama and tragedy out of their own neediness for contact with her.

Being one-dimensional is deadening for us and others, and yet we cling to our image or stance as if it were a life preserver, as indeed it is. Sharon won't let go of drama and tragedy until she trusts that her deeper, varied self is indeed capable of inspiring the connectedness she so deeply wants. Our novelty is, in the end, what connects us to ourselves and others, and our novelty can only survive when we let go of our familiar, habitual patterns.

The stance we take is established on a physical, intrapersonal and interpersonal level. I have commented on how Sharon used tragedy *inter*personally to insure connection. *Intra*personally she was organized in a way which resulted in her seeing or creating the suffering aspect of living wherever she looked. She became anxious when she saw or connected through other stances for very long, because she had little support for being free of burden. Physically she looked burdened—slightly bent in her back as if she had a weight there. When, in the therapy hour, she would allow herself to uncurl upwards in her back and upper body, she would momentarily feel the excitement of being open and free, but soon would feel overexposed, as if someone was about to ridicule her.

Terry, who had a similar character to Sharon's, described herself as being like a mule, the beast of burden. In one session she played with the opposite image of being a race horse. Allowing herself to be the race horse in fantasy, she could imagine prancing, freedom, and speed. She couldn't allow herself to be the race horse, i.e. get out of her chair and prance, that day, as that felt too exposing, but a seed had been planted for her internal race horse to begin to stir.

Through introjection and projection, defined earlier, we lose the race horse and are left with experiencing *only* from the standpoint of a mule.

Examples abound in my everyday life and practice of the phenomenon of image development and maintenance.

Jim is an example of someone who had come to an image of introspection and introversion thru the loss of his natural curiosity. He had been encouraged to repress this resource through the introjects of "Mind your own business," "Don't look," and "Curiosity killed the cat," in a family that was excessively private in even the most basic life functions and information.

Swallowing those injunctions, he began to take less interest in the outside world—physically averting his eyes, holding his tongue and holding back his exploration. Over the years the loss of outside stimulation had become habitual for him to the point of forming the image that he was inherently independent, a man who needed no one. He not only had that image of himself, he prided himself on it.

The difficulty he had in sustaining such an image was the frequent depression he suffered and a vague sense of loneliness. In therapy I noticed how infrequently he simply looked at me, and when he did so it was as if he really did not see me. I asked him one day to begin experimenting with his eyes, to soften them and look around as if he were absorbing the room through his vision. He did so with some pleasure, but noticed that he wasn't truly looking at me. As he began to explore me visually, he began to feel the tightness in his jaw and upper body that accompanied the old admonition to stay back and not invade another's privacy. I assured him that I felt no sense of being invaded, and this gave him enough support to begin the experiment of reowning his curiosity and his visual ability to satisfy it.

If we sustain enough loss of ourselves, or if we specialize too much around who we are (e.g.; tragedy queen or introspective, sensitive man), we are likely to self-substitute by identifying ourselves with the more peripheral aspects of life. There is an exercise I have done with my students from time to time that helps elicit a sense of what one is relying on for a sense of identity. It is a simple exercise in which two people pair off and one person asks the other, "Who are you?" The other person responds with the first words that come to mind, then the question is repeated. Examples of responses that often come from such an exercise are "I'm a mother, I'm a man, I'm a homeowner, I'm a student, I'm intelligent," etc. These are all words we use to establish an identity and are represented in the following diagram:

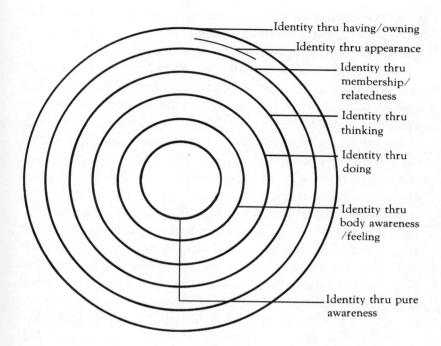

Identity thru having/owning

Identity thru appearance

Identity thru membership/relatedness

Identity thru thinking

Identity thru doing

Identity thru body awareness /feeling

Identity thru pure awareness

I have drawn this symbol of identity to represent the most superficial ways of self-identification (owning, having) to the deepest sense of self (feeling and pure awareness). All of the rings add to us and our identity, but as we go inward in the diagram we are on increasingly firmer ground. Let's look at each way of knowing our selves.

OWNERSHIP, THE HAVING SOLUTION

Acquisition is an exciting human experience. To see or find something that pleases us and to purchase it for all the future pleasure it promises, adds a lot to our lives. In addition to the excitement of acquisition, our material objects can offer us daily pleasure and a sense of security and permanence, particularly if we continue to notice them after the initial excitement of purchase wears off.

As a major factor in our identity, however, ownership and materialism have some inherent dangers. The first is that overidentification with things leaves one exceedingly vulnerable. If I am my money or my things, I risk losing myself if life strips me of my belongings. In the depression of the 1930's, many people who overidentified with their money jumped out of buildings because, when they lost their things, they in effect lost themselves.

Overidentification with materialism is also dangerous in that it can lead to a life scenario of acquisition to gain a greater sense of wholeness. If I am my money, then when I have more money I am more, and when I have less I am less. A pattern of hoarding, calculating, and competitiveness comes out of such an orientation, as each transaction represents not exchange, but a potential reduction of self.

Finally, an identity which rests on possessions requires huge amounts of effort. We must work to make money for the original purchase, and then spend time and money maintaining it. If it is of high value or we are particularly attached to it, we will likely insure it, which will require more money (and the time to earn it) for the premiums. With this kind of attachment we will likely spend a good deal of our life energy worrying about material loss, and if we have many possessions this territorial watchfulness may become a powerful undercurrent in our lives.

Eric Fromm once said that being is reduced by having. I believe he was referring to these traps. What we own can wind up owning us.

Jeff grew up in a poor family in which he felt the sting of humiliation frequently. He was humiliated by bill collectors harassing his family, and by his home which was substandard in comparison to those of his friends.

Humiliation is a powerful experience for anyone, and Jeff spent a great deal of his adult energy avoiding it by climbing the corporate ladder. He had an outstanding salary, and owned many nice things, but he still felt anxious, as though he had not put enough distance between himself and his humiliating, poverty-stricken past.

Jeff is an excellent example of how we use our life stance to avoid our feelings. He used acquisition and wealth to put humiliation behind him, but humiliation was still present. It was simply in check. Each time we approached that humiliated little boy within him in therapy, he would find reasons to terminate, and often would do just that. Fortunately for Jeff, he had enough insight and strength to come back after a rest. Acquisition is a nice addition to living, but not a very satisfactory substitute for it. To regain life and aliveness Jeff needed to reconnect with some of the pain he was avoiding.

APPEARANCE, THE IMAGE SOLUTION

If we grab onto material possessions to save us from a limited sense of self, we likely do so out of a concern for an image we have created—an appearance. Advertising encourages an image orientation to life, and many of us are ripe to swallow new images to fill the emptiness within.

Physical appearance is closely related to the materialism of our cars, clothes, houses and lifestyles, as all these appear on our surface, on what is outermost in our makeup.

Clare was lamenting that she wasn't more voluptuous in a recent therapy hour. Her husband frequently expressed disappointment that her breasts weren't larger, and would often comment on the bodies of women who had fuller figures.

I asked her to close her eyes and picture her husband. As she did so she could feel anger rise within her, and she expressed it in fantasy.

After her anger completed, she was left with a feeling of softness, and out of this softness came the words, "I'm more than that (breasts), much more." We were both touched by the quiet shift that had taken place in that moment, a shift to an identity that went far deeper than appearances or expectations.

As with possessions, our appearance adds sweetness to our living. We all appreciate seeing someone whom we consider "beautiful." And we want to show ourselves off to best advantage with our new hairdos, clothes, and tans. It's fun, and it's part of adding beauty (ours) to the world.

But in the end, it's not *us* in any deeper sense, and if we limit identity to outward appearance, we are again vulnerable as the years go by and time mirrors our changes. We are our appearance, but, as Clare said, we're more than that—much more.

MEMBERSHIP AND RELATEDNESS

Often in the "Who are you?" exercise, presented earlier, responses revolve around connections to others. "I'm a mother" or "I'm a father." I'm a Robertson or I'm a Mac Elroy. Interpersonal relatedness is certainly an important aspect of identity, but it is easy for many of us to lose a sense of individuation as we emphasize relationship to others.

Don is an example of this trap. This was evident when I asked him in what way he was important or substantial in the world. He said he was only important to his family, a response which defined him in terms of belonging. In other sessions we had discovered that he almost always defined himself in relation to others. He had very little concept of himself individually.

To expand on his sense of identity, I asked him to imagine that he was the last person on earth (to exclude relatedness). In this fantasy he had everything he needed, and life, except for the absence of people, was like he had always known it.

As he proceeded through this exercise he moved from experience to experience and, although he felt lonely and empty intermittently, he recognized the pleasantness of non-people-related activity. In the end he had two other ways to know himself and to validate his importance. He identified himself as an explorer and musician.

We are members of the human race and to any subgroups to which we belong, but we are more than that as Don was beginning to discover. An important rhythm between individualness and merging with others is a central issue for us all.

THE INTELLECTUAL SOLUTION

I have described earlier how, when we give up parts of ourselves, we fill up the created void with mental constructs. We begin to live in our heads, creating many "home movies" as life substitutes. The intellectual solution underlies much of our ego image, and is a major source of loss of contact. If I have given up my natural curiosity, as Jim had, I will move more and more into my head to satisfy my need to know how things are. I will abandon attempts to get to know you and will subsequently tell myself a story about who you are. Likewise, abandoning my own feelings and responses will result in my establishing a story (images, rationalizations, roles) about myself and my life. Thoughts, thoughts,

thoughts. Thoughts about who you are, who I am and how it (life) is. This imaging extends to the creation of our unique self-image.

> But this image is not who we are. Rather, it is like a map of where we have been in the past, and not a very good map at that, for it is constructed of abstractions based on only a handful of our thousands of life experiences. The map is not the territory, proclaimed Alfred Korzybski, and so the map of the ego image is not the territory of the actual self. Consequently, as long as I persist in identifying with this map (as many people do much of the time), I know myself only as an abstraction, rather than as a self, alive and real (Olney, no date).

We lose much when we mistake the thinking we do, the stories we create, for life itself.

ACTIVITY, THE DOING SOLUTION

Particularly in the American culture, activity is favored over simply being and experiencing, and one can keep himself away from feeling physical sensation and true contact with the world by the sheer quantity of one's activeness. When we over-identify with our achievements, our improvement, our production and "getting someplace," we don't allow time to savor and absorb. Space and emptiness are necessary elements in deepening experience, but an emphasis on production often precludes such a stance. Rollo May addresses this avoidance when he says that, "It is an old and ironic habit of human beings to run faster when we have lost our way" (May, 1969). Societally, we are an action generation. Do more. Feel less.

The last two sources for identity, feeling and physical sensation, and pure awareness will be the subject matter for the latter chapters of this book. The sources of identity thus far described are avenues for feeding our deeper self, but the danger is that owning, appearance, interrelationships, thinking and doing often become a substitute for it. Reliance on the less substantial aspects of living results in going for long periods of time without being fully present. It is as though we are not really living our lives, and to the degree that we're not experiencing the moment, this is an apt description.

To live most fully anything we do must be brought back to our internal experience, or we will continue to feel incomplete—an incompletion which will demand that we simply continue to buy, achieve, obsess or distract ourselves again. As we attempt to be more present, however, we will discover the glue that keeps us avoidant. An ingredient of the glue is the unconscious illusions that keep ineffective life patterns in place.

7

The Underlying Illusions

Each role or image we maintain, each behavior or life-style that diminishes our life, is based on an illusion to which we cling. The American College Dictionary defines illusion as "a perception of a thing which misrepresents it, or gives it qualities not present in reality." These misrepresentations were established in childhood when we didn't have the maturity to interpret what we observed into clear, rational, personal truths that would give us positive direction in creating our lives. Unexamined, these illusions stay with us into adulthood, unconsciously serving as maps for daily movement.

THE SCRIPTS WE MAINTAIN

One of the most common illusions that we carry is that being who we truly are will not result in specialness—that organically we're not enough. We're taught this when we are often judged as falling short and by a future orientation to living. This is reflected in the question frequently asked of children, "What do you want to be when you grow up?"

(when you become a real person). The torture rack of self improvement to which many of us lash ourselves is the result of this orientation as we constantly quest to become someone as opposed to finding the someone we are.

When I would ask Julie in a session to sit and experience herself on a feeling level, she would soon become distracted and restless, saying this wasn't enough. I asked her to say the sentence "I'm not enough," and when she did, she felt a sudden rush of anger. The anger—when focused on, became directed at her father who was never satisfied, her father who always had another goal for her to complete. There was seldom a time she could remember when he sat with her, simply being with her as she was.

When I was with her in this way, the old illusion rose again. "My feelings, my essence, what comes spontaneously from me is of little value. Certainly not enough to keep someone's attention." She had observed her father's turning away from her in the moment in favor of a future expectation, and had concluded that she simply wasn't enough. The truth that eluded her was that her father had a problem. He couldn't stay with his own feelings or with his daughter's for any significant length of time.

Because we are often unaware of our illusions, we are not free to challenge them. Each of the case examples in this book are based on an illusion of some kind—an assumption that life is the same today as when the illusion came into being. Roger, in Chapter One, assumes that if he gets close to people, particularly women, that someone will expose him in a humiliating way. Janet, in Chapter Two, has the illusion that women are less than men, so that to identify with her womanliness automatically means diminishment. Both Dick in Chapter Two and Laurie in Chapter Three, have the illusion that expressed aggression will be punished by a source of aggression bigger than themselves. And finally

Mary's illusion (Chapter Four) is that the only way to feel cared for is to maintain the attention of those in her immediate environment. The following is a list of illusions some of my clients have carried.

Examples of Illusions

1. Conformity leads to security.
2. We can earn love.
3. Expressed anger will result in loss.
4. Surrender will lead to invasion.
5. Independence requires giving up one's need for warmth/support.
6. If I'm good, I will be treated well.
7. If I'm not loved, I'm unloveable. If I'm alone, I'm unloveable.
8. There's something wrong with me.
9. That Self Acceptance will result in changelessness.
10. The strength of need is the measure of the strength of love.
11. Polarities cannot exist within us. We must be consistent.
12. There is a "right" way.
13. I am my thoughts; I am my image.
14. To preserve a relationship I must remain unknown.

The list of illusions is endless. Irving Yalom, in his book *Existential Psychotherapy* (1980), describes a favorite illusion of one of his clients. It is the magically held belief that if you refuse the loan (life) you won't have to pay the debt (death). A client of mine presented an illusion when she stated, "I can't stand rejection." Some have the illusion that they can't stand alone—others that they will lose themselves if they connect.

There is a grain of truth in all illusions that increases their hold on us. If I don't live fully, if I don't take risks, I may increase my longevity. There *are* people who won't stay connected to me if I don't perform or produce. Rejection is difficult to take and can wound one's spirit. Some people will attack me on occasion when I express myself or move toward what or who I love. It is also true that we can't stand alone entirely, that we have a natural interdependence, and likewise true that others may insist on our imprisonment when they become involved with us.

But the partial truth becomes self-destructive when it begins to represent the whole. The bell tolls for all of us whether we play it safe or go for the gusto. Rejection, although painful, is not life threatening, and if received clearly, can be life enhancing. Although it may not be one's preference, standing alone can be experienced, weathered, and may even become a pleasurable stance. And finally, we can begin to see others who don't love us for who we really are, and allow them a new place in our life, or no place at all.

What we are more likely saying with our illusions is that we haven't learned how to "be" with the avoided experience. My client who said "I can't stand rejection," was more clearly saying "I haven't learned how to be with it." It is, of course, legitimate for her to go further and say, "and I don't want to do the work of finding out." By rewording it thusly, she reduces the distortion of the illusion; she makes it a choice and regains herself as a life creator. It's hard for many of us to let go of pleasing, hard to work out freedom and connectedness, hard to stand alone or to ask for help. Life is hard. Our illusions cloud its difficulty by implying impossibility.

THE BENEFITS OF BEING ASLEEP

It would seem that, if there is a promise of fuller living for each of us, we would all be actively seeking the path toward that end; and yet, though we give growth lip service, most of us defend against self-actualization. We defend to protect ourselves, to stay with what is familiar, to stay with experiences at a level we can support. This is wise. We must honor our defense against life as much as we honor our desire for it.

As we begin to experience our defenses, it is often clear that we are primarily defending ourselves against what is within. There is a great deal of energy and power in each of us, and when it manifests through feeling and physical sensation, it can be frightening. This can be especially so when, through therapy or other powerful life experiences, feelings which have been long held in check begin to emerge. Sadness, love, anger, excitement, joy and sexuality can feel overwhelming if we have not developed support for, and comfort with these feelings over the years. We also need to protect ourselves from the outside world. Just as we defend ourselves from too much internal stimulation, we need to block out or blur incoming sensory input that is excessive.

Reducing external stimulation came up humorously in a group therapy session. I had given Sarah several bioenergetic exercises to try, and the result was that she felt very grounded. "Grounding" is a term that bioenergetic therapists use for a strong sense of connection with one's body and a strong feeling of being supported by one's lower half and the ground below.

As she stood there I asked her to look around the room and see what life was like from this stance, a stance of being solidly present. She felt the pleasure of it in the protected environment of the group, and I suggested she might experiment with it in everday life. She burst out in a youthful way and said, "Oh, no! That would make life much too vivid!"

We need to give ourselves breaks in this fast moving, modern world. We need to deflect some of the incoming energy. We need to shield ourselves, distract, and "space out" until we replenish our strength for contact. Sometimes we need to avoid enlivening interaction until we learn more effective ways of supporting our vitality.

Related to this inner and outer reality, avoidance is a desire to avoid "existential givens." These are the truths that are inherent in living, truths that can be hard to bear: our own finiteness and the finiteness of those we love. Our own separateness, personal responsibility, and choice. Our ultimate powerlessness in the most important aspects of living, and the basic meaninglessness of living short of the purpose we create.

Finally, we maintain the status quo of our life habits until we are ready to make room for, or take a stand around, new information. Awareness pushes for action, and until we have the energy to create and activate, we may keep ourselves ignorant. Old habits, prejudices and judgments simplify life and make it easier and more efficient. Newness takes time to assimilate. Sometimes there is too much to do to commit to staying in touch.

In the rhythm between needed safety and desirable expansion, we each find our pace. The wonderful discovery that comes to most self-explorers is that the safety that heretofore has come from defense and distortion can come from greater contact with what is true. We can know the truth and the truth, arrived at with self-acceptance, can indeed set us free. It is to rediscovering our personal truth that we will now turn.

Section III
The Road Back to the Self

8

Self Recovery

In spite of the many protective advantages of maintaining the status quo, there are many who opt for the difficult and rewarding journey of deep personal self-exploration. For some, the initial motivation is in terms of symptom reduction, e.g. alleviating depression, anxiety, substance abuse or acute crisis. For others it comes out of a need to become clear before making a choice. Still others initiate inner work in the hope of discovering greater aliveness, greater depth of feeling, more authentic relating, or spiritual connectedness.

PERLS'S MODEL OF NEUROSIS

Regardless of the initial motivation for beginning, the process and direction of one's work, for me, is the same. It is based on becoming acutely aware of ourselves at expanding levels of our functioning and existence. Perls gave us a useful model for these levels in the following diagram.

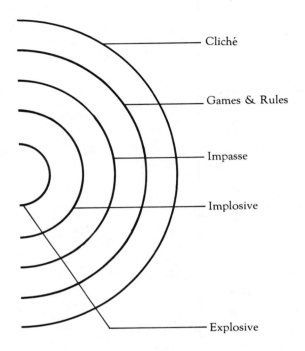

Cliché

Games & Rules

Impasse

Implosive

Explosive

In this model the cliché layer is the easy standard of living that we use to conserve our energy and deintensify action and interaction. "Hello, how are you?" Asking when one has little interest. Smiling out of custom. Making conversation. This mode of being demands little of us and, thus, is a conserving stance. The next level serves some of the same purpose. We have already described it in earlier chapters. It is the stance of identifying ourselves with our professions, roles, a favored kind of behavior, or thoughts we create about ourselves. It is the ego image and gives us comfort through consistency.

Increased awareness at these outer levels can lead to a great deal of energy release and pleasure. It comes when we identify the clichés, games or roles that we play or that we hold in check which leak out half-heartedly. Paul was an example of this in a training workshop I led several months ago.

> Paul was aware of how frequently he took center stage. He had a high need for applause which he tried to hide because of his own and other's criticism. At this level of experience he was often the showoff (under cover) to receive the approval he needed.
>
> As his work unfolded I asked him if he would be willing to step into his showoff and actively attempt to get the approval. He agreed to do this and, as we were meeting in his house, his guitar was fortuitously at hand. He chose to show off by playing and, as he did, his increasing excitement was apparent. Showing off uncriticized can be extremely enlivening. His audience, other members of the training group, gave him a great deal of applause as well as laughter, as we all recognized the showoffs in ourselves.

Is it clear how awareness and increasing our identification with a stance can render it harmless at any level of functioning? When I engage in cliché behavior with awareness, it feels completely different. When I am doing my serious, observing role with awareness, I can experience my energy shifting toward greater pleasure. When Paul became the showoff, the showoff that he had submerged, he became free, and interestingly, people who had previously resented his attention demands softened considerably. Awareness in any of these examples does not mean getting rid of the role or game; it simply means experiencing it. Its staying or leaving will come out of awareness. At this level of existence we don't decide how to be; rather our task is to discover who we are.

Fritz Perls's writings have a more critical slant to the outer layers of character than I am comfortable with, although if he was alive today he might well agree with the premise of Dick

Olney's work in Self Acceptance Training. Dick states that the goal of therapy (and I believe he would agree with any self-exploration) is to disidentify with the ego image, to replace my self-evaluation with the awareness of what I really am behind the screen of self criticism. Self-evaluation and criticism in Perls's model rests in the outer area of games and roles. We create, through thought, an image of who we are and who we are not and maintain it through more thought in the form of defenses.

Self-acceptance, of course, does not exclude our self-evaluation ability. Self-evaluation in the service of one's well being is a central resource in self-refining, clarifying and maturation. What *is* thwarting and destructive is self-criticism and the kind of excessive self-evaluation which obliterates the experiencing of whatever I am in the moment. This obliteration often comes in the form of inner questions, as Olney puts it. Questions like, "How am I doing?," "Am I doing it right?," "What are they thinking of me?," "Am I living up to my ideal self image?," "How can I protect myself from future catastrophes?" It's difficult to truly experience oneself intellectually, physically and emotionally amid the clatter and constraint of such an evaluative symphony.

If we are able to let go of some of the self-evaluation, and are able to take a step or two back from the games and roles that comprise our self-image, we have the beginnings of possible change. What we will have done is to create a space—a space that was once filled with rules, maps, cause and effect relationships and body postures. It's called the "impasse" (p. 100). It's an empty space that can be experienced as no-thought, non-attachment, confusion, despair, relief or freedom. Many feel it physically as a hollowness in their belly or chest. In a sense it's a space we've created by re-evaluating our lives, throwing out the useless, stopping our distractions, letting go of old patterns and seeing more clearly what actually exists.

It can be a difficult time when we are "in-between" without our usual supports. A client of mine reflected this difficulty when she seriously considered breaking a ten-year-old pattern with her husband. They had a dominating father/compliant daughter relationship as the basis for their marital union, one in which she likened him to a hammer. She was the nail. When she began to turn away from his direction, though, anxiety began to set in. She expressed this in one session as "not knowing what to do or how to be."

The last sentence reflects the doing orientation held by so many. In truth, how to be or what to do is less dependent on a conscious decision-making process than on what naturally unfolds from us on its own. This is not to say that we don't make choices in what we allow ourselves to express, but rather that who we are isn't what we do, but how our unconscious energy comes forward. If one stays with the above-mentioned empty space, subtle feelings and sensations will, over time, emerge. Much of this newness will reflect what we disowned along the way.

So we can see the impasse as a kind of incubation period as we wait to see what comes up. More poetically it can be seen as a rebirthing, what we give birth to is a new, more complete sense of ourselves. Reflecting on Perls's diagram of our character structure, we can imagine how the imploding layer is a description of how we keep ourselves in. This happens on a physical level and on a thinking level. It is what Freud described with the words suppression and repression. If we begin to let go of chronic constrictions in our body, or confront and let go of outdated ideas in our mind, or move differently in life, the explosive layer will have more opportunity to release. Perls encouraged us to not be afraid of the word "explosion," as he meant by it an energy force by which we would consistently come out to the world in a lively manner. For Perls the primary forms of this kind of explosion erupt into feelings of sadness, joy, anger and orgasm. The important concept here is that we have awareness of what has been lost. What we do with it is secondary, although important, in the completion of our gestalts.

THE GESTALT MODEL FOR HEALTH

The more we confront the kind of awareness process described in this book, the closer we come to the ability to move, relatively uninterrupted, through clear gestalten. Gestalten are patterns or forms that have a natural wholeness. Thus if we move through life completing what emerges from within and what confronts us from without, we will often have a sense of well being. The following illustration represents such a process in living.

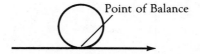

Point of Balance

In this illustration the circles represent gestalten. On a here and now level they might reflect hunger and its satiation, tiredness and its satisfaction through rest and restlessness, and its completion through movement. This pattern completion is life itself, as needs, feelings, ideas and direction become foreground, become satisfied and return to background, setting the stage for the next emerging gestalt. The ability to move "uninterrupted" through the gestalt is the key concept to insure health. It is akin to Dick Olney's encouragement to become self-accepting, which he describes as "experiencing myself physically, intellectually and emotionally in any present moment, without the inhibition of simultaneous self-evaluation, self-criticism or self-judgment." Both Perls and Olney put a great deal of trust in uninterrupted human nature. Gestalt work has an optimism to it that rests on the premise that each of us has an inner, positive-directed, pro-life wisdom. This wisdom has various labels. Gestalt therapists call it "organismic self-regulation."

Organismic self-regulation describes a belief that our physical being has within it a natural ability to know what it needs to stay in balance. Moment by moment, if I am truly in touch, I can move in ways to promote optimal health. Stan Johnson, a physician, echoed this sentiment when he wrote, "Every action we take, moment by moment, tends to promote either balance, integration and health, or imbalance, conflict and disease" (Johnson, no date).

Gestalts on a mini, immediate level can be completed in a relatively short period of time. For instance, as I sit at my typewriter I feel the need to stretch, and after leaning backward over my chair (completing that gestalt) I return to my typewriter. As I finish the last sentence I have a need to review something written earlier and so I read, returning to write after absorbing an important idea. And so I go on and on, as do you. These kinds of foreground/background shifts reflect the constant adjustments that we make during our days and nights to give ourselves support, comfort and accomplishment. The more we hone our ability to attend our process, the better we are giving ourselves all three of these things.

Out of the immediate flow of gestalt resolution come larger gestalts of longer duration. The circles in the above illustration could represent patterns that take years to complete. Developing a place in a community, achieving skills in a profession, creating intimacy in a relationship are all long-term gestalts. Of course there are many sub-gestalts within such life endeavors—places for us to feel completed, places in which we can rest, places in which we can turn to another focus. One's total life is, in a very real sense, a large gestalt, one which is completed only when our life is over.

Larger gestalts are less spontaneous of course, requiring more self-containment, discipline and focus. This is difficult for those who have disowned or never developed impulse control nor learned the pleasure of containing energy for the promise of greater satisfaction in the future. One description about such a lack is reflected in the following quotation.

> I did not want to see the connection between the magnificence of her (the dancer's) art and the torturously hard work she had to do to accomplish it . . .
> I shouldn't have to work for recognition . . . the idea that I should actually have to exert myself for my accomplishments was humiliating . . . (Quote from unknown source)

Athletes discipline themselves routinely as they develop their excellence through disciplining their movement, developing strength and keenly experiencing their natural rhythm. Musicians do likewise. Such people give up some aspects of living to develop depth in another. I recently read an article which quoted Bruce Springsteen as saying that his sister was more talented musically than he, but was too popular to develop her talent. In an ironic way his lack of popularity as a teen allowed him the space, without distraction, to be with his music and to take the gestalt of music to higher levels.

It is important to remember, though, that life development according to the model presented in this book comes originally from our experiencing the moment and addressing emerging gestalts. When I notice myself in daily activity, notice when my excitement or interest arises, I may have some sense of my true vocational direction. When I experience my unique needs clearly on a daily level, I begin to have a correct sense of myself and the kind of marital relationship that would work for me. Likewise, I will gain a sense of appropriate lifestyle development, friendship patterns, recreation interests, etc.

Finally, attending to the moment's emerging gestalt is important in a way which bypasses the larger gestalts mentioned above. It is expressed in the saying, "It's not so much what you do, but how you do it." It's not so important what kind of work one does, but whether one is able to involve himself in work in a way that integrates one's inner world with the demands of the workplace. In relationships this concept would mean, within reason, that it's not so important to choose the perfect partner. More important would be one's ability to maintain a sense of self within a relationship, and know something about the process of merging two gestalts in a way that nourishes both. Expanded, this theme holds that the better we get at acknowledging our gestalts and supporting their completion, the less we rely on the environment for our sense of well being. Out of this kind of maturity we can transform, and to some degree, transcend outer reality.

9

Sharpening Gestalts

Both Gestalt Therapy and Self-Acceptance Training include teaching as a part of the therapy experience. The teaching is focused on awareness as an important part of rich living. One of the exercises is called the "awareness continuum." It is a simple exercise of noting one's awareness verbally from moment to moment. To start such an exercise one begins each sentence with the phrase "Now I am aware of . . ." We are always aware of something even if it is a blankness, and so the continuum goes on and on and we begin to make discoveries about how we are organized in the world.

Awareness can be categorized into three areas. The first area of awareness is external. We use the senses of sight, smell, touch, taste and hearing to receive our immediate surroundings. The second area of awareness is internal and is comprised of our felt sense. A felt sense may include emotions, but is not limited to them. It is a total sense of what one is at that moment in time on a body level. The third area of awareness is what Perls calls the "midzone." It is the area of our thinking: conceptualizing, comparing, planning, worrying, and remembering.

In doing the awareness continuum, one may readily get clear as to how much of his life is devoted to attending to life versus creating a sublife in his mind. I sometimes refer to this sublife as our propensity to create home movies. Although not necessarily bad, spending time in the midzone can be life-avoidant if done to excess. If done more consciously, however, one can be more in charge of its usefulness through greater awareness.

The awareness continuum is the basis for much of the work that I and other gestalt therapists do. Patricia Baumgardner underlines the importance of this technique when she describes, "introducing and reintroducing the awareness continuum." She says that,

> It takes time for people to learn to be involved and to discriminate between experience and intellectualization, or between what is oneself and what is the other person. It has been my experience that until he reaches this point (of discrimination and awareness continuum) the patient is simply unable to make use of all the rest that Gestalt Therapy offers. Once he masters the awareness continuum, he knows how to work. He has achieved a basis for being responsible for himself and letting be, for continuous discovering, and for communication (Baumgardner, 1975).

We can increase the amount of uninterrupted here-and-now contact in our lives by reducing the midzone connection. To the degree that we are successful in that effort, our organismic self-regulation will have a greater voice in our direction. It's a different kind of living when we come from clear contact. It's the kind of living that Stanley Keleman describes in the following way:

You don't have to know, you don't have to search out an answer or find a way. That's the mistake most of us make. We are looking for knowledge, for a ready-made way, instead of letting our feeling and our self-expression form our way (Keleman, 1975).

Increased awareness may be used in three primary ways to approach the kind of living that Keleman encourages: developing perceptual contact, softening the repressive hold, and experiencing preference. They are simple ideas that can take a lifetime to incorporate.

DEVELOPING PERCEPTUAL CONTACT

The first way has to do with the quality of our contact with the outside world. Our ability to feel deeply, to allow emerging gestalts to sharpen, relies heavily on our willingness to let the world in through our senses. Are we willing to let the world impact us? If so, the sight of a beautiful woman or a handsome man will stir us in some way, music will influence our mood or prompt us to move, smells will draw or repulse, taste will satisfy or disgust, and touch will please or repel.

There is no more graphic way to think of the impact of our senses than to consider how they arouse our feeling during lovemaking. Simply the thought of using sight, taste, smell, touch and hearing with one's partner in a lovemaking fantasy can be stirring, let alone being present for such an experience. If one makes love with few interrupting thoughts, the sexual charge can be enormous and discharge through orgasm brings completion. Contrast this in your mind with an individual who has limited use of his senses, or interrupts his senses frequently with thought, during foreplay. His/her charge will be significantly different in quality and quantity.

A full emotional, physical and cognitive experience requires full participation, and this, in part, relies on making good contact with the environment.

As we increase the use of our senses, we will be greeted with both positive and negative sensual experience.

> Ken was attempting to allow more passion in a lifeless marriage, but when I suggested that he begin to use his eyes more in relation to his wife, he became resistant. In exploring his reluctance it became clear that when he used his eyes to see her, he became aware of feelings of disgust. This was particularly evoked by her female body.
>
> This kind of disgust is not at all uncommon. We have a society that promotes sexual imagery at the same time it discourages familiarity with, and appreciation for, our physicalness.
>
> Treatment for Ken consisted of helping him to tolerate his disgust and gradually desensitizing himself to his wife's physicalness through brief periods of greater sensory awareness. We also looked at the source of his introjected, critical attitude. As of this writing he is aware of less disgust arising in contact with his wife, and just the beginnings of a new sexualness and desire in relation to her.

Another client, Doug, had a different kind of difficulty in using his senses with his wife.

> Whenever he would look at his wife, he would begin to compare her with his ideal image of the way a woman should be. She didn't match his pictures, and, in the process of thinking about her in this way, he lost touch with any attraction that might have happened.

Both men have blocks against making solid contact with women. They are defending against an openness that is required to fully experience the opposite sex. This is true for Ken because he has swallowed an attitude, and for Doug because he has learned to approach women in a strongly evaluative manner. When any of us begin to approach the world in a less heady way, we can expect discomfort at times. We repressed sensual experience for a reason. We may discover that reason as we regain it.

Awareness and enlivening the senses through attention and discipline is one way of increasing contact with our surroundings. Another way is to create and maintain novelty in our lives that will naturally spark the senses. We notice the novel while we become habituated to, and unaware of, what is constant. The most obvious source of novelty in our lives comes from the changes we make. We change cars, houses, jobs, towns, music, clothes and marital partners to reawaken interest and aliveness.

The less obvious source of novelty comes from our ability to perceive subtle changes that exist only for the attentive. Our surroundings seem the same because we have ceased to look, listen, smell, taste, and hear. We unconsciously and consciously assume we "know" our surroundings because they are familiar, but our mental habits block our ability to perceive the fact that we are always changing.

This issue arose for me when my wife and I celebrated the ten-year anniversary of our first date. We spent the evening repeating what we had done ten years before—racquetball, a hot tub and dinner.

As the evening wore on I became a bit nostalgic, longing for the feelings that accompanied what we had experienced years before. Not that I wanted to replace the deep love we have for each other now, but I wanted the deep love and the innocent freshness too.

I woke up the following morning with a possible answer to my longing. In order for me to have the feelings I desired, I must find a way to be fresh, to be with my wife as if for the first time. To do that I must leave my program of "knowing her" and try looking for and finding the new woman that she is every day.

When I said this to a friend the next day, he teased me about heavy philosophizing, which was partly true. But the fact is that my wife *is* different every day, as is the world. We love the innocence of children as they explore their new world. How can we reown that in ourselves, and recognize novelty in the process?

There is a spiraling effect to the process I am describing. When I look more closely I become aware of even more to see. I begin to understand new levels of receptivity, as I pick up more refined nuances. I can know more deeply the smells of those close to me, the variations of taste in my food, the textures of clothes on my skin, the range of voices in my daily life, and the patterns of shadows that come in different seasons. Very few of us have exhausted the possibilities that are present in our current environment. Thus novelty is very close by.

SOFTENING THE REPRESSIVE HOLD

The first focus for developing better here and now contact had to do with our openness to the world around us. We are now turning to the second obstacle to contact which is called "repression." I am using this term to describe a body/mind attempt to rid from consciousness certain attitudes, feelings or body sensations. Ken, recently mentioned, illustrates this concept. He swallowed an idea about the female body (developed a mind set), and subsequently learned to avert his eyes (a muscular set) when in the presence of a woman. He also learned to tighten his diaphragm so that he would not experience the disgust which was unpleasant to him. He was left with an unconscious orientation with a symptom of passionlessness in relation to the opposite sex.

Each introjected thought and each projected part of ourselves has its representation in the muscular skeletal system of the body and vice-versa. This truth is extremely important in personal growth and overall well-being. It means that new insight or a change in thinking can, and does, affect physical experience. A shift in musculature or posture likewise affects thoughts and self-concept. It is important to work with both systems, mind *and* body, to produce meaningful and lasting change.

> As I worked with Louise she began to notice a hunchedness in her upper body. Her shoulders were rounded and her diaphragm was restricted. She was discussing her many problems, and how life seemed so difficult—a theme not uncommon for her.
>
> As we sat together I commented on the regularity of this stance, how frequently she had a companion, a problem on which to focus. An extremely lonely woman throughout much of her life, she had created a kind of familiar friend to whom she could turn.
>
> I asked her to dialogue with "problems" and her worked turned into a kind of saying good-bye to this aspect of her living. As she came to the sentence, repeated several times, "I don't need a problem," her breath began to expand and there was a noticeable shift upward in her chest and upper torso. She began to feel waves of feeling which she described as feeling free.

Reduced repression can come about through cognitive re-evaluation. Louise was able to allow the thought that she might not need to create problems when they didn't exist. This is evidenced in many forms of therapy and is one way of entering the body/mind system. Less well known are attempts to know oneself (and ultimately change) through physical focus and alteration. This is ironic because, when we notice someone has changed, it usually has less to do with new thoughts and more to do with a change in their energy, aliveness, movement or physical expression. Here is an example of thoughts shifting in relation to physical change.

John had been depressed off and on throughout his life and had come into therapy after a particularly difficult time of depression and stuckness. He had very little sense of his body, but was aware, when it was pointed out, how little movement he had in his chest. His breathing was barely perceptible.

In one session he expressed interest in exploring his anger. He knew it was there, but he never was quite able to feel it fully. He had had some bad luck in the past year, so I asked him to focus his anger on fate as he swung a tennis racquet into a pillow. His breathing and chest movement became fuller as he allowed himself to "have a tantrum." He was perceptively more alive when he set the racquet down, but within a few moments could feel his critic begin to chide him by saying, "So what, you threw a tantrum, how does that change anything?"

The critic has a point. In effect, throwing a tantrum as an adult does not often have a desirable effect on the outside world. But there are two important changes that did take place. The first was that John had changed. He felt less stuck and was perceptibly more alive. Through beating a pillow he had freed up his energy, which, beyond momentary embarrassment, gave him a great deal of pleasure. Secondly, and perhaps more importantly, in the following weeks John began to experience more aggressive energy in resolving some of the environmental stumbling blocks which confronted him. Once energy is free and available, the problems of living take on a whole new light.

The physical aspect of repression is reflected primarily in chronic muscle tension patterns in our bodies. We contract to reduce or eliminate experience that we cannot support. Often the experience that is eliminated is one of feeling— feeling that, if recognized or expressed, would threaten (or seem to threaten) our survival or well being. The threat can be internal because our feeling can be a powerful force and may frighten us. Or the threat can be interpersonal as our expressed feeling in the past may have been met with censure, ridicule or punishment. Either way, we control physical experience or feeling by controlling or reducing our movement. Full feeling requires full body movement, and if movement is arrested, premature cessation of feeling is assured.

In order to reverse the repressive process, awareness must first be brought to the unique ways that we each have of blocking strong energetic experience. These patterns of blockage will be evident in three major body segments. The first is comprised of the head and neck; the second the torso, including the chest and abdomen; the third is the supporting segment of the pelvis and legs.

Tension and misalignment found in any of these areas can be worked on through awareness, physical exercise and experimental movement. If I make a physical shift (allow my breath to come in and out more fluidly, or let go of tension, for example), I will experience myself differently, and this difference will often be an expansion. With the difference will come memories, feelings, and ideas which add to the material from which we are organizing new life. For example, breathing into a chronically tight belly may allow sadness and

longing to emerge—feelings which may have long been held
in check. Allowing greater chest expansion may result in a
feeling of greater openness and receptivity. Allowing a tightly
held jaw to slacken may prepare us to claim long repressed
anger, and allowing greater pelvic movement while walking
can set the stage for greater sensualness and sexuality.

Working with a body orientation is particularly effective
because the body is less adept at defense. We have all learned
to use our minds to hide to some degree, and so one's
intellectualizations are prone to be obfuscating. Body work
allows for the surprises—the new, healing truths to come
forward. Entering a person's organization through both
mind and body levels, however, is the most powerful vehicle
for self discovery and change. They continually complement
each other in the self-exploration process, and, over time,
integrate toward unity.

EXPERIENCING PREFERENCE

Natural wants arise out of making more contact with the
external world and allowing greater feeling to develop from
within. These wants and preferences, and the attempts we
make to satisfy them, give life its direction as our gestalts
open and close. Allowing wants and needs is the third area
that one needs to strengthen to allow for the sharpening of
gestalts and their completion.

On a rudimentary life level, wants and preferences are
defined as needs, and our autonomic nervous system provides for us in its miraculous wisdom. This was graphically
demonstrated to me during a stress test physical I took
recently. While on the treadmill, but before running, I
glanced up to see a digital instrument which was monitoring
my heart rate. It read 52. I felt touched as this was, for me, a

close contact with my heart, which provided for me day and night. I began to play with my heartbeat by meditating, opening my eyes to see it slow to 48. Opening my eyes brought it back to 50 and as I returned to normal conscious-ness it went back to 52. Minutes later, as I ran on the treadmill, my heart rate climbed to 60, 70, 80 . . . giving me just the amount of blood circulation I needed for my level of physical activity. This is an example of baseline organismic self-regulation. Barring physical illness, structural malfor-mation or chronic tension, our heart (and other organs) gives us exactly what we need.

As we progress towards higher levels of functioning, our wants and needs become more subject to interference and interruption. The next level of gestalt completion includes our spontaneous responses to those around us and our environment. The smile of joy when we see a friend, the angry expression when we feel abused, and the reaching out for support when we feel depleted are all examples of spontaneous emergence and wanting. In the first two ex-pressions (joy and anger) there is an unconscious desire to communicate, to show others what we feel inside. In the last example we are involved in a more complex gestalt, as we show our exhaustion *and* reach for support. Uninterrupted, all three represent a completed gestalt: contact—internal stirring—movement to the outside world.

As gestalts and wants become more complicated, they may be more difficult to discern and satisfy; and there may be the added complexity of competing gestalts. Nevertheless, one can become more adept and clear in experiencing preferences in such varied activities as eating, resting, sexual desire, exercise, accomplishment, observing, initiating, cre-ating and destroying. In Eastern philosophy the sage, when asked his "miracle," responded, "When I am hungry, I eat, and when I am tired, I rest." This is a simple personal philosophy based on individual rhythm and the pleasure that is derived from matching internal want with external gratification.

Improving perceptual contact, working to allow greater sensation within the body, and defining with sensitivity one's wants and preferences are all building blocks for a more creative life. Out of knowing *what is*, internally and externally, our lives begin to unfold in a way which more truly reflects our uniqueness, our changingness and, in the end results in our contribution to the world. For many of us psychotherapy has been a useful experience toward increased authenticity, creativeness and realness.

10

Therapy and the Therapy Hour

THE THERAPIST'S CONTRIBUTION

The road to self, to greater aliveness, is a difficult one. It goes through our habits and defenses, which once were our supportive friends, but which, over time, have outlived their usefulness. Each of us has the desire to live as fully as possible, and yet we sleep protected by the status quo. Openness to ourselves and to life outside ourselves is difficult, and it frequently helps to have a companion—a friend who can teach, observe, help and support while inner strength develops. It is for such a relationship that one turns to a therapist.

The teaching in such a relationship is primarily oriented to giving the client new ways of experiencing themselves, a process of awareness and self-acceptance. This kind of life stance can be learned. In fact, Dick Olney defines his work as Self Acceptance *Training* (emphasis mine). It is not a kind of learning which tells others *how* to be, quite the opposite. It is a kind of learning which helps us discover how, and who, we *are*.

As an observer in the client/therapist relationship I use my senses and my inner feeling to acknowledge the obvious—not the obvious, solely or primarily in terms of what I analyze or think is true, but what I can note, in the present, as my client and I sit together.

Early in my sessions with Rachel I became impressed with her accomplishments. She had gone to a prestigious college, had had a successful career and now, in her sixties, was a consultant to a variety of groups on aging.

As I sat with her in our fourth session, an image of a shining star came to me. It occurred to me that she was, indeed, a star. I shared this with her and she laughed self-consciously, a recognition reflex for what she knew to be true. I reflected back to her her physical response, and we began to explore her brightness and how she had learned to hide her shining talent in reaction to historical admonitions. By the end of the session her self-consciousness had subsided to some degree and she was able to say, "I'm a star," with an excitement that was almost beyond her body's ability to support.

Rachel was a star and my recognizing it and helping her to consciously acknowledge it led her to increased feeling that comes through self-acknowledgement.

Keenly observing and intuiting is part of how a therapist can be helpful to a client. The therapist can also offer broad knowledge gained over the years about human issues and help clients recognize self-destructive patterns around existential themes. He can be of help in offering them experiments to try (in the therapy hour or outside of it) to deepen experience or expand alternatives.

Robert, a sensitive, soft spoken man, was working with me in marital therapy. As he and his wife began a session, he off-handedly related a recent work experience in which he had been chided for not showing enough aggression. He somewhat sarcastically closed the story by saying he wasn't Lee Iacocca (Chrysler's board chairman).

Later in the session Karen, his wife, was describing how she was punishing Robert for something that had happened a year before they were married. Robert sat listening with a submissive posture. I asked him to show me how Lee Iacocca would handle his wife's complaint and he virtually rose up out of the chair saying, "O.K. I messed up, you have a week to drop it so we can move on."

This new stance was electric to both him and his wife as they burst into laughter. There's a little of Lee Iacoca in all of us.

Help from a therapist can come from many sources. Observation and experimentation are two. Help through clarifying illusions, establishing historical impediments to fullness, and shifting body posture are others. Underlying all of these, however, is the support that a therapist gives throughout the self-exploration process. The experience of a client spending fifty minutes being the center of another's focus is an important part of that support. Although it may be difficult at first to receive that kind of attention, it is a luxury that is seldom afforded most of us in everyday living. We seldom pay that kind of attention to ourselves, let alone have it from someone else.

As I listen carefully to clients they begin to listen more carefully to themselves. Carl Rogers, one of the first humanistic psychologists, had this process in mind when he developed Client Centered Therapy. The basis for this listening, for him, came through the realization "that it is the client who knows what hurts, what directions to go, what problems are crucial, what experiences have been deeply buried. . . ." With this orientation he goes on to say that unless a therapist has "a need to demonstrate his own cleverness and learning, he would do better to rely upon the client for the direction of movement in the process (of therapy)."

This kind of listening to, and attitude toward, the client is the underpinning of a refining process that takes the client deeper and deeper into himself. "I experience this, no that's not right, it's more like . . . yes, let me be with that a moment. . . ." It's the refining, finding our immediate subtleness, that is enlivening. It also makes us unique and therefore an addition to those around us.

Safety is an essential element for such self-listening to take place. For disowned parts of ourselves to emerge, trust through acceptance must be present. Since, in most cases, the client can't provide all the self-acceptance necessary, the therapist lends the client acceptance while self-acceptance develops. For effective therapists this acceptance of clients is not a technique, it is an orientation, an openness to clients as they are. It is born of delving deeply into their own process and those of their clients over many years. Criticism of others comes partially from knowing them superficially— not understanding them in a broader and deeper context. Acceptance comes more readily, in my experience, when one has the luxury and orientation of knowing someone more fully.

THE THERAPY HOUR

Each therapy hour is a fifty-minute opportunity for here and now exploration. It begins with attention being paid to what is foreground for the client and what the client wants out of our time together. When I use the term "foreground" I am primarily addressing how a person experiences himself on a feeling level—what is his sense of the energy within.

When I ask what they want from our session I am asking for a beginning focus and intent. Both are extremely important in the kind of living we have been talking about (what are you feeling and what do you want?). Good therapy is a microcosm of the world at large, and clear gestalt formation and completion is the basis for therapeutic work.

At first blush the question, "What would you like from today's session?" sounds innocuous enough, but for many this here and now statement of preference and hope is difficult. Although we are continually making choices, we infrequently experience ourselves as the chooser. When the choice process is a focus, it can be revealing and powerful. What do I want here? What will I choose? What fits for me today?

The question is also relationship defining. It suggests, as Carl Rogers stated, that clients know what's best for themselves. That they know what's timely, what direction to take as they evolve. This stance also implies that clients are responsible, that they need to be active in remembering their dreams, noting meaningful interactions during the week, and pay attention to feelings and rhythms that evolve. Many wish to avoid that responsibility by seeing the therapist as more powerful, wiser, knowing them better than they know themselves. A stance of elevating the therapist, like any other, needs to be owned, accepted and examined; but therapy progresses more rapidly the more one becomes an active member in the exploration process.

Gail seldom had an answer to the question of what she would like from our session. I pointed this out and asked her to sit with this lack of preference for a while. She agreed and brightened as she recognized that she did have one. She wanted me to lead, to simply "take her on a journey."

I asked her to imagine my doing just that, and she saw me taking her by the hand and leading me down a country lane. She was filled with easiness and peace as she gave up responsibility, something she rarely surrendered to in life.

Paradoxically, Gail took responsibility by giving me responsibility. We all organize differently around the issue of wanting, but no matter what the personal variance, it is a central gestalt to address. Rollo May (1969) suggests that, indeed, the core of therapy is enhancing a client's ability to want deeply. Our wanting, attraction and desire reflect a deep part of our being, and, as such, lend themselves to feelings of vulnerability. When a client comes forward with what she wants as Gail did, she is revealing herself below shoulds and intellectualizations. This requires trust—self-trust and trust of the therapist. It's a trust that can be encouraged, but more profoundly comes at its own pace, unchosen and uncontrolled.

As therapy progresses virtually anything can serve as a beginning focus: a pending decision, an emerging feeling or its absence, problems of interpersonal connection, addictions, a dream or a need to rework issues in one's history. Equally as valid is to begin a session without an issue, without a beginning focus. Without an agenda the beginning focus for a session will be simply the client's inner or outer awareness.

Carol came to our session with no agenda, and so I asked her to do the awareness continuum described earlier. Her response was that she didn't want to do it, that it was "too hard."

Now, of course, it is important for any client to have full support for refusing any experiment, so I seldom push for cooperation. It is also important to explore resistance, and so I asked her to elaborate on her "it's too hard," response. I asked her to do this elaboration in a particular manner, however. I asked her to focus on her body to get a felt sense of it. Gendlin (1978) describes this way of experiencing:

> A felt sense is not (just) an emotion, and focusing is not a process in which you "face" painful emotions nor one in which you sink down into them and risk drowning. Conversely, it is not an intellectual or analytical process either. When you learn how to focus, you will discover that the body, finding its own way, provides its own answers to many of your problems.

Carol and I had done focusing before so she began to focus, giving her body time to speak. She felt some fear and, as she stayed with it, the words, "I'm afraid I'll blow it" blurted out.

It was a beginning, but the natural question is, "blow what?" She described how in such a wide open process (the awareness continuum) she might say something that would offend me or result in a reduction of my caring for her. So, in essence, Carol's refusal to do the offered exercise was her attempt to be careful, to not risk losing my positive regard which had become so important to her.

This brief focusing example highlights two important parts of Carol's character. The first is her idea that my (and other's) care for her is fragile and could be easily "blown." The second, growing out of the first, is that to preserve important relationships she must be very careful. In Carol's case this results in her being excessively rigid, guarded and often withdrawn. Her rigidity also makes her less emotional and more anxious, the latter being her original reason for coming to therapy.

There were clear historical roots for Carol's seeing relationships as fragile. Her relationships with her parents while growing up were fragile, particularly with her father. Connection with him *did* depend on her being careful, especially careful not to disagree or be different. Given a choice between being spontaneous and assuring her connection with him, she chose the latter as she loved and needed him very much.

In subsequent sessions Carol began to feel anger at having given up so much of her own vitality to insure relationships. She began to notice this process when it was happening, and could interrupt it to her benefit. Most affirming, she discovered that most of the people in her present life were quite accepting of her spontaneity. Several even commented that they found themselves enjoying her more.

Another session illustration involves Ann, a woman who had been in therapy with me for several years. She came into this particular session with no agenda, but quickly noticed her chest was constricted when I asked her to focus on her body sensation. Now, tightness in any part of the body is often an attempt to say "no" to something—no to letting something in (as when a child tightens against a hypodermic syringe) or no to something emerging from within. Ann suspected that something was trying to form internally and that she was fighting it.

I asked her to tighten her chest even more and she said she felt like a cement statue. I asked her about her life as a statue and she replied that she was strong, could be leaned on and had no feeling. When asked what kind of feeling was best to be without she immediately replied, "hurt." Now she and I knew what she was repressing, and as she came to this insight she began to cry softly. Asked to tell me all the people who hurt her, Ann listed them and her crying increased. Several times during her list she would begin to tighten against her

feeling, twice beginning to get angry. I encouraged her to
return to her hurt, not because anger is illegitimate, but
because we were working with the softer gestalt of hurt and
broken heartedness and I didn't want to interrupt one gestalt
with another. Ann had much less difficulty with anger. She
had always been an angry fighter, but it was her sustained
softness and vulnerability that eluded her.

As her hurt deepened and her tears came, she remem-
bered her mother's sarcastic admonition, "There you go
crying again, you'll just become a puddle of tears." I
suggested that she become just that, and she spread out on
the floor, letting herself be the puddle her mother obstructed
through humiliation. Her crying continued for a while as she
let go of the chronic muscle tension in her back, the tension
that kept her away from softer feeling but ready to fight. For
now she had given up fighting the tears that are an important
part of living. For now she had a new way of experiencing her
body. It takes a great deal of energy to maintain a "fight
ready" stance, and there was a great deal of pleasure in the
momentary "giving up."

Each of these case vignettes demonstrate several ways of
reuniting with lost experience. In Carol's session the path of
work was more intellectually insightful, touching on emotion briefly at certain points. We used our relationship as a
bridge to understand her communication patterns with
others, and deepened the insight by revealing its anchor in
developmental history. Intellectual understanding is, by
itself, useful as an initiating point for change, and is often an
important step in a path toward a feeling-oriented focus. It is
also, as demonstrated by Carol, an important part of becoming aware of anti-life behavior patterns and the estab-
lishment of alternative reactions.

Ann's work made use of intuition and feeling as a path
toward deeper experience, and physical movement. As a

result she has, over a period of time, allowed herself to sink into her body as an initiating point for experience and movement.

Each client poses a unique configuration of organization, a pattern which can become known through time and careful attention. It is my job to study each of them with enough freshness to discover their specific, unique gestalts in important areas of living. It is also my task to develop a method of self-exploration that my client can use. I take both of these challenges seriously as a source of delight and a life-long commitment.

SECTION IV

MERGING BEYOND THE SELF

11

Intimacy, the Self and Others

As we experience ourselves more completely, we will often have the urge to share ourselves with others. To the degree that we have achieved a deep sense of ourselves, intimacy and communalness is possible. By definition intimacy is a sharing of the self and the receiving of another. The more I allow of myself into consciousness, the more I will have to share.

As my self-awareness and self-acceptance increase, they form a solid base from which I can make solid contact with the world. This solid ground allows me to relate to others without unconsciously losing myself in the process. It also allows me to withstand any attempts by others to overrun me.

From the stance of grounded self-awareness my partner, children, friends and community become part of my external sustenance, adding to my well-being without defining it. I experience them as the icing on the cake, but do not confuse them with the cake itself. My experiences of myself on a body level represent the more sustaining ingredients of my existence. At this level *I* am the cake, an integration of all that is in me.

With this greater sense of identity I can come into a relationship in a less dependent manner and avoid the common trap of trying to remodel my partner to better fit my needs. Out of this orientation good contact evolves. I am in touch with who my partner *is*, not who I want my partner to be. Because I am aware of the wide variety of humanness within me (and accept it), I am less surprised by, or opposed to, the humanness I see in others. I can often extend self-acceptance to include others.

Abraham Maslow (1968) described this high level of relating as "need-free love." Anne Morrow Lindbergh (1955) captures some of its essence in the following:

> Relationship is strangled by claims. Intimacy is tempered by lightness of touch. We have moved through our day like dancers, not needing to touch more than lightly, because we were instinctively moving to the same rhythm.
>
> A good relationship has a pattern like a dance and is built on some of the same rules. The partners do not need to hold on tightly, because they move confidently in the same pattern, intricate but gay, swift and free, like a country dance of Mozart's. To touch heavily would be to arrest the pattern and freeze the moment, to check the endlessly changing beauty of its unfolding. There is no place for the possessive clutch, the clinging arm, the heavy hand—only the barest touch in passing. Now arm in arm, now face to face, now back to back—it does not matter which, because they know they are partners moving to the same rhythm, creating a pattern together, and being invisibly nourished by it.
>
> The joy of such a pattern is not only the joy of creation or the joy of participation, it is also the joy of living in the moment. Lightness of touch and living in the moment are intertwined.
>
> One cannot dance well unless one is completely in time with the music, not leaning back to the last step or pressing

forward to the next one, but poised directly on the present step as it comes. Perfect poise on the beat is what gives good dancing its sense of ease, of timeliness, of the eternal.

Solid identity allows us to be light with our partners, and at the same time gives us the foundation we need to risk merging with another. Erich Fromm (1941) had this in mind when he wrote,

> That man, the more he gains freedom, the more he becomes an individual, has no choice but to unite himself with the world in the spontaneity of love and productive work, or else seek a kind of security by such ties with the world as destroy his freedom and the integrity of his individual self.

A dance exists for all of us between being highly individual and merging with those around us. Held onto too tightly our individuality renders us impotent. It precludes the kind of commitment to something outside ourselves that we need to thrive. Striving for intimacy, for an integration between myself and another, has many interpersonal subrhythms, issues that become steps in the dance. As each are addressed in the moment, a couple, quite literally, creates a rhythmic movement unduplicated in time. Let us examine a few of the steps that go into each couple's unique dance.

SIMILARITY AND DIFFERENCE

Fritz Perls was fond of saying, "Contact is the appreciation of differences." When difference can be appreciated it offers us the variety that completes our lives. My maleness is complemented by having a female partner and female friends.

My slowness and tendency toward receptivity is enhanced by having friends who are quicker paced and more prone to action. My talents are limited and I can enjoy and rely on the talents of those around me. Even with personal expansion I can only be a limited version of the human experience. Vicariously enjoying the differences of others is a way for me to extend myself beyond my life experience.

Beyond the excitement and stimulation provided by difference, is the opportunity to learn from another's different style, pace, interest or viewpoint. Other people can expand our perspective, and remind us, in a positive way, of forgotten and unused potential. We can, by modeling and active encouragement, be useful to each other in deepening and expanding life experience.

At the other end of the polarity, difference can, at times, be grating. The amount of difference can exceed our tolerance level. We may be depleted and simply not want to bump into or be faced with stimulation that doesn't blend with our immediate set. There is a safety and a comfort in being with like-minded, like-behaviored others. Agreement and similarity give us a haven, a confluence.

Perls's admonition stressed developing our ability to be with difference, to allow it to enliven us. I believe this injunction came out of an observation of our overconforming, homogenizing tendencies. Equally important, however, is our ability to provide for sameness, for similarity when the time is right. When we are in a space of limited capacity for difference, we must be able to ask our partners to shift to our rhythm or be willing to break contact with them until reconnection is possible.

This issue of similarity and difference is a part of all the issues that follow. In earlier chapters we focused on how differences within us could live together and integrate. The question in intimacy is how differences between two separate people can come together in a whole relationship.

DEPENDENCE AND INDEPENDENCE

When the foundation of a relationship is based on individual responsibility, when there is no *claim* on one another for support, there is considerable room for dependence, independence and interdependence within an intimate connection.

Because our strength and skill development is always in process, always incomplete, we want and need the assistance of others. Dependence can be relationship enhancing. It is one form of human connection. If I can let go of my adult competence momentarily, I can allow my child-like vulnerability to come forward. In relationships this can mean allowing another to take care of me, take care of my life's burdens for a time and allow me time and space to recuperate. If I can say to another, "I'm depending on you," without a controlling intent, I'm allowing myself to experience their importance to me. At the same time I'm allowing them to know it. This can be difficult for many of us when we've had hurtful experiences with felt dependency. Joe is an example.

Joe's mother died when he was five years old. His father was not interested in child rearing and there was no one to turn to to meet his five-year-old needs for help and assurance. His solution to this dilemma was to close off to his needs to receive from others, and he became the "little grown up" on whom others could rely. We often do for others what we want for ourselves.

Joe's dependency disownership resulted in a great deal of depression during his childhood and early adulthood. He was depressing anger at his father for forcing him into premature adulthood. As he worked in therapy he got in touch with his five-year-old desires and began to seek out relationships that could support this part of him. Depression then lifted significantly and he became more expansive, enlisting the help of others in fulfilling his dreams and plans.

Interestingly enough, as he began to depend on others, he began to experience some bouts of anxiety—anxiousness that he had felt years ago when his mother died. In one session, as he attended to an anxious feeling he was having, the sentence, "Who's going to take care of me now?" emerged. The answer to that five-year-old's question is that the care can come internally *and* externally. He couldn't do that for himself at five without disowning his body, and there was no one there to hear his need or intuit it. Now there is (or can be). He is free to search himself for the kind of strength he needs, and search his environment for the kind of people on whom he can rely.

On the other side of the dependency/independency continuum is the pleasure that comes from being leaned on, being the strength for another's need. To allow another to lean, one must have a sense of their own strength or talent. Being dependable for another person demands a sense of commitment, an ability to focus one's energy (and aggression if necessary) on a stated goal. When all of these characteristics come together, the statement, "you can depend on me," is possible. It is an expression that is often accompanied by a feeling of delight and solidness.

There is a delicateness to dependency in an intimate relationship. It can cross over into controlling interaction quite easily, which runs counter to the light touch we encountered in Lindbergh's words. There is room for controlling another in a good relationship, but it is my belief that it should be used sparingly—only on those occasions where not having control poses a major threat. This premise is evident in the following couple's interaction:

> Tony and Jennifer lived monogamously, but opted not to make it a relationship rule. At one point in their marriage, however, Jennifer was feeling particularly vulnerable and approached Tony requesting a promise of monogamy. He thought about her request, but refused. He was, by nature monogamous, but making it a rule felt wrong to him and an impasse ensued. Jennifer dealt with it by escalating saying she couldn't continue their relationship unless he concurred with her request.
>
> Tony stewed with this ultimatum for a day or so, not wanting to lose his stand or his relationship with Jennifer. He finally offered to promise fidelity until Jennifer was able to deal with her vulnerability and return to a position of strength. In effect, he was letting her depend on him (his commitment) until she felt more independent. She agreed to a one-year promise of monogamy, and the exchange was concluded.
>
> Three days later Jennifer, somewhat shyly, approached Tony saying she was feeling better and no longer needed his loaned commitment. In effect she used his promise, an outside structure, until she felt her strength return, and it was a statement of her integrity that she used it no longer than it was needed.

Borrowing support from our friends, family or lovers reminds us of who is ultimately responsible, and allows us to experience the gifts and giving that are a part of interpersonal exchange. They may be loans that we rely on for a lifetime, and our appreciation for the gift can remain lifelong. However, once loans become rights, or gifts become taken for granted, intimacy and merging through a deep love is in serious jeopardy.

NURTURING AND BEING NOURISHED

Nurturing takes many forms. There is the loving look, the home cooked meal, the light touch in passing, clean sheets for one's guest, the mended shirt, the washed or repaired car, relaxed conversation, or the friendly expression, "How can I help?" The essence of each of these is based on the nurturer's desire to bring pleasure to the nurtured (and subsequently to himself through their delight), and to be willing to work for their well being. As such it is a dynamic interaction between two or more people which depends on the ability of each to experience the desire to nurture or the ability to receive it. The old adage, "It is better to give than receive," has no relevance in what I am describing here. It is not better to give or receive; it is useful and fulfilling to have access to both.

There are a variety of ways that openness to our own capacity to nurture is thwarted in our developmental history. At times it is blocked by others focusing on us, exclusively. We introject their focus, learning to orient only to ourselves, and lose the richness of experiencing sensitively the world around us, tending to needs and deficits that we observe. At other times a desire to nurture is extinguished because it is accompanied by a trap.

At the beginning of our session, Jane said, that she had become aware of the desire to please me, and that she wanted to get over it. I asked her simply to say, "I want to please you" and see what emerged for her. After saying it several times she could feel a choking, trapped sensation in her upper chest and throat. She asked me if, when I wanted to please someone, I felt as if I were at their mercy. I said, "Not that I remember, but the point is that this is true for you." Wanting to please and being under someone's control went hand in hand.

As it turned out, her father had used her desire to please him against her while she was growing up. It's a simple and common thing to do. He and many other parents do this in the following stance: "If you want to please me, don't *do* this, don't *feel* that, don't *be* that way." Used excessively with little regard for a child's uniqueness, the message is, "if you want to please me, you must be like me," or "you must complete the picture of how I think you should be."

When the desire to please and nurture is paired with a demand to give up important aspects of our essence, we can do one of two things. We can close off to pleasing, or we can become "pleasers" with a reduced sense of ourselves. In adult reality, however, we needn't choose one or the other. We can learn to nurture and please *from* a sense of who we are.

On the other side of this issue is our degree of comfort in receiving gifts in any form. Just as wanting to give can trap us as children, receiving nourishment can place us in an untenable position. Many gifts come with hooks. This was true for my client Joyce in the triangle involving her father, her mother and herself.

Joyce had difficulty in our relationship over time as she felt my acceptance and warmth toward her. The more she allowed herself to experience my caring the more anxious she became. The anxiety had a sense of impending punishment, as if she were "going to have to pay a price."

In her childhood Joyce's primarcy source of love and joy was in her relationship with her father. An irresponsible man, he was open-hearted with his daughter, but in constant conflict with his wife.

Joyce quite naturally gravitated toward her father as we all do toward a source of love. There was a bind in receiving this nurturing, however. It came from her angry, competitive mother. She would scream, "If you go to him, don't come to me." What was Joyce to do? To receive love from her father was to risk losing her mother. Love was not free, but potentially very expensive. Her resolution throughout life was to seek love from men, but to become anxious when it came, which ultimately sabotaged her relationships.

Once we begin to evaluate how the simple act of giving and receiving nourishment can be entangled with irrelevant side issues, we can become more available to our natural nurturing rhythm. The issue becomes an interpersonal one of how nurturing will be expressed in a particular relationship. How does my partner best receive nourishment? Where and when do they need it most? What would make it easier to let in caring? How can I ask for that? How can I expand ways of being nourished, and giving it? Intimacy thrives on a good resolution of this issue. Life can be depleting, particularly when it is lived fully. To have sustaining relationships that add to us is a blessing.

Other issues in relationships include control and submission, sharing and privacy, contact and withdrawal, and individuality and merging. Each is an area for individual exploration and interpersonal sharing and integration. They are best resolved with the hope that there is room in the relationship for the fullness of each member, and that each partner can learn to commit to the well-being of the other. An acquaintance of mine had a slogan written on his wall which read, "What is good for Diane (his wife) will eventually be good for me." It is a simple way of noting that one person's growth eventually returns to nourish another's well being.

BEYOND ISSUES

An interesting thing begins to happen when a mutual commitment is the basis for a relationship. The issues mentioned above become less and less charged, less and less important. They may be topics for conversation throughout a couple's history, but each of the categories mentioned represents structure, and structure becomes secondary to letting go into experiencing each other in the present. It's a merging sensation that goes beyond words. It goes beyond explanations, categorizations and attempts at control.

Structure in relationships, and in life as a whole, is useful in that it provides a support on which merging can later rest. It is useful to think of the basics of interpersonal interaction and discuss them so that one can choose a partner who is on the same path, and is committed to a similar journey. It is also useful to use the structure to get clear about blocks intrapersonally and interpersonally. But the larger goal is to use this structure to reach for the ultimate goal of loving deeply. Otherwise one simply has compatibility. Anyone with soul practices his form, his technique, his basics so that he can eventually leave the mechanics and ride the crest of unstructured pure experience. It's true of an athlete, an artist, or a craftsman in *any* kind of work. It's also true of lovers as they begin to lose themselves, the selves they work so hard to find, in the process of merging with one another.

12

Merging Beyond Humanity

Thus far the emphasis of this book has been on becoming more deeply aware of oneself, particularly on a body level, to allow for the completion of emerging gestalts. On a worldly level this process is the basis for our experiencing the pleasure that accompanies a free flow of energy within us. In the last chapter I discussed a gestalt which is characterized by a desire to let go of self and its boundaries and to merge. This merging is at least partially satisfied through love and service to others, but, in a self-reflective life, a transpersonal path is often needed. Carl Jung knew this when he wrote in *Memories, Dreams, Reflections*:

> Only if we know that
> the thing that truly matters is
> the infinite
> can we avoid fixing our attention
> on futilities and upon
> all kinds of goals which are not of
> real importance. . . .
> If we understand and feel that
> here in this life we already have

a link with the infinite,
desires and attitudes change.
In the final analysis,
we count for something
only because of the essential we
embody, and if we do not
embody that,
life is wasted.

If we return to the circle figure that represents an emerging and completed gestalt (p. 104), we note that in a full circle there is a place of balance, an empty place which is available for the next gestalt. It is also available for continued emptiness if we learn how to support and nurture such an experience.

This empty space is a deeper way of knowing ourselves, even deeper than the rich experience of living from one's body awareness. It is the space that Deikman (1982) describes as the "observing self" and is represented in the identity diagram on page 83. In a sense the observing self, our pure awareness, is our spiritual essence, while the body is the deepest manifestation of our earthly being.

Deikman offers us a simple way of tapping into this place within us when he suggests that we, "Be aware of what you experience visually, then close your eyes. Awareness remains. Behind your thoughts and images is awareness, and that is where you are."

This is the place that Eastern philosophy encourages. It is a receptive orientation that is absent of intent. Thus it is accompanied by a lack of tenseness, strong feeling, or a need for activity. It is a receiving place without thought or judgment, and as such, is an addition to the Western way of dynamic action.

There are a number of ways to encourage the emergence of this observing self. The awareness encouraged throughout this book often brings one naturally to it. When we truly experience our bodies from moment to moment, we are very close to the underlying pure awareness that we are discussing. Sitting or moving meditation training also brings one in touch with this cosmic sense of ourselves. Learning to be increasingly open hearted is another path. All of these stress an ability to expand beyond an earthly plane, to be able to step fully into experience without holding back an objective foot. In this kind of living we must learn to experience life directly.

This kind of experience is thwarted by all the defenses described throughout this book. The defenses are primarily mental constructs born of greed and fear, and are geared to keep us asleep to the existential realities of life—the reality that life is change; the reality that change will eventually destroy everything earthly; that one cannot possess anything; that everything is on loan. My wife, Ginger, keeps the following words posted in full view, in an attempt to keep our family awake:

> Living a full life is a constant rehearsal
>   for giving up one's life.
> Eventually we must give up all which
>   is precious to us.
> It is a simple existential reality.

If we bring the truths of existence continually into our awareness we begin to live differently. We can begin to practice the Eastern sage's encouragement to be involved without being attached. That is to say that we can have our life just as it is, but we must avoid the clinging. Clinging and grasping is an attempt to avoid loss, to maintain the status quo. If we can accept the loss, described in my wife's quote, we can stop trying, in our minds, to keep life the same and begin to experience it as it is *now*. Stephen Levine (1982) caught this spirit in the following story:

> Once someone asked a well-known Thai meditation master, "In this world where everything changes, where nothing remains the same, where loss and grief are inherent in our very coming into existence, how can there be any happiness? How can we find security when we see that we can't count on anything being the way we want it to be?" The teacher, looking compassionately at this fellow, held up a drinking glass which had been given to him earlier in the morning and said, "You see this goblet? For me this glass is already broken. I enjoy it, I drink out of it. It holds my water admirably, sometimes even reflecting the sun in beautiful patterns. If I should tap it, it has a lovely ring to it. But when I put this glass on a shelf and the wind knocks it over or my elbow brushes it off the table and it falls to the ground and shatters, I say, 'of course.' But when I understand that this glass is already broken, every moment with it is precious. Every moment is just as it is and nothing need be otherwise."

Stephen Levine goes on to say that,

> "When we recognize that just as that glass, our body is already broken, that indeed we are already dead, then life becomes precious and we open up to it just as it is, in the moment it is occurring. When we understand that all our loved ones are already dead—our children, our mates, our friends—how precious they become. How little fear can interpose, how little doubt can estrange us. When you live as though you're already dead, life takes on new meaning. Each moment becomes a whole lifetime, a universe unto itself."

Viewing life in the way that Levine encourages requires that we cultivate our observing self. It is a stance of involvement without attachment and will mean that we attend to the process of living without undue regard for the result. As a tennis player I am with my movement and the rhythm of the game, and less concerned with the score. As a therapist I focus more on being with my clients, open to their organization, and am less concerned with a predetermined desired result. Because I trust my process and my clients', I have less need to control myself or them.

When we find a way to live life from the two innermost places within us, the body and the observing self, we are in the truest contact with who we are. The outside world becomes less important in determining our sense of happiness and peace. To the degree that we are able to center deeply on who we truly are, we are free. Although we may enjoy the outer trappings of living, we are not dependent on them and we don't confuse them with who we are. We can be happy in a cave or a castle.

What I have just described is high living. We can't *wish* it to be true, or it simply becomes another swallowed introject. We can, though, through attention, self-acceptance, courage and personal work, become sensitive to the magic that already resides within us. We can also learn to notice the magic that surrounds us. This book was one path for me to relearn the things I need to know more deeply to accomplish that end. May it be of use to you in your journey toward life's miracles.

Bibliography

ADLER, ALFRED. *Understanding Human Nature*. Greenwich, CT: Fawcett Publications, Inc., (1927) 1969.

BANDLER, RICHARD & GRINDER, JOHN. *Frogs into Princes*. Moab, UT: Real People Press, 1979.

BAUMGARDNER, PATRICIA. *Legacy from Fritz*. Palo Alto, CA: Science and Behavior Books, 1975.

DEIKMAN, ARTHUR J. *The Observing Self: Mysticism and Psychotherapy*. Boston: Beacon Press, 1982.

ERIKSON, ERIK H. *Childhood and Society*. New York: Norton, 1950.

FREUD, SIGMUND. *A General Introduction to Psychoanalysis*. New York: Washington Square Press, 1952.

FROMM, ERICH. *Escape from Freedom*. New York: Rhinehart, 1941.

GENDLIN, EUGENE T. *Focusing*. New York: Everest House, 1978.

HOUSTON, JOHN P. *The Pursuit of Happiness*. Glenview, IL: Scott Foresman, 1979.

JOHNSON, STANLEY L. *To My Patients*. Privately published, 1977.

JUNG, CARL. *Memories, Dreams and Reflections*. New York: Vintage, 1961.

KELEMAN, STANLEY. *Your Body Speaks Its Mind*. New York: Simon & Schuster, 1975.

LEVINE, STEPHEN. *Who Dies?* Garden City, NY: Anchor Books, 1982.

LINDBERGH, ANNE MORROW. *Gift from the Sea*. New York: Vintage, 1955.

LOWEN, ALEXANDER. *The Language of the Body*. New York: MacMillan, 1958.

LOWEN, ALEXANDER. *Betrayal of the Body*. New York: MacMillan, 1967.

LOWEN, ALEXANDER. *Depression and the Body*. New York: Penguin Books, 1972.

LOWEN, ALEXANDER. *Pleasure*. New York: Penguin Books, 1975.

LOWEN, ALEXANDER. *Bioenergetics*. New York: Penguin Books, 1975.

MASLOW, ABRAHAM H. *Toward a Psychology of Being*. New York: Van Nostrand, 1968.

MAY, ROLLO. *Love and Will*. New York: Norton, 1969.

OLNEY, DICK. *The Perennial Therapy* (unpublished article).

ORNSTEIN, ROBERT. *The Psychology of Consciousness*. New York: Harcourt, Brace and Jovanovich, 1972.

PERLS, FRITZ. *Gestalt Therapy Verbatim*. Moab, UT: Real People Press, 1969.

POLSTER, ERVING & POLSTER, MIRIAM. *Gestalt Therapy Integrated*. New York: Brunner/Mazel Publishers, 1973.

REICH, WILHELM. *Character Analysis*. New York: Simon & Schuster, 1945.

ROGERS, CARL. *On Becoming a Person*. Boston: Houghton Mifflin, 1961.

YALOM, IRVING. *Existential Psychotherapy*. New York: Basic Books, 1980.

About the Author

Jim Doak was born August 22, 1945. He was raised in the San Francisco bay area and graduated from California State University, Chico, with a B.A. degree in 1966. He received his Master's degree in Social Work from California State University, Sacramento, in 1968, and has been a practicing psychotherapist since then. His post-graduate education includes training with the Gestalt Institute of San Francisco (1973-1976) and with Dick Olney and Cherie McCoy in Self-Acceptance Training (1979-1983).

In the beginning of his career Jim worked in a community mental health setting and as a staff member of the University of California, Sacramento Medical Center (1972-1976). During his employment with the Medical Center he was a Graduate Field Instructor for the University of California, Berkeley, and California State University, Sacramento. During that time he was also a Clinical Faculty Instructor for the University of California, Davis.

Since 1976, Jim has been in full-time private practice. He currently has offices in Sacramento and Nevada City, California. In addition to working with individuals and couples in the self-exploration process, he trains other therapists in Gestalt Therapy and Self-Acceptance Training. He is currently an Associate Member of the Gestalt Institute of San Francisco.

Jim is married and has one son. He enjoys skiing, tennis, running and playing the fiddle. This is his first book describing his therapeutic practice.

David Bedford was born in Devon, in the southwest of England, in 1969.

David wasn't always a writer – first he was a soccer player! He played for two teams: Appleton Football Club and Sankey Rangers. Although these weren't the worst teams in the league, they never won anything! David was also a scientist. His first job was in the United States, where he worked on discovering new antibiotics.

But, David always loved to read, and he decided to start writing stories himself. After a few years, he left his job as a scientist and began writing full-time. He now has over 15 books published, which have been translated into many languages around the world.

David lives with his wife and two children in Norfolk, England.

Keith Brumpton has written and illustrated over 35 humorous books for children. He also writes scripts and screenplays. Keith lives in Glasgow, Scotland.

For Ali and David, for all your
help and guidance.
DB

First American Edition 2006
by Kane/Miller Book Publishers, Inc.
La Jolla, California

First published in 2004 by Little Hare Books, Australia
Text copyright ©David Bedford 2004
Illustrations copyright ©Keith Brumpton 2004

Library of Congress Control Number: 2006920744
Printed and bound in China
1 2 3 4 5 6 7 8 9 10

ISBN-13: 978-1-933605-06-7
ISBN-10: 1-933605-06-5

DAVID BEDFORD

Illustrated by Keith Brumpton

Kane/Miller
BOOK PUBLISHERS

Chapter 1

Harvey's fingers trembled as he handed over the money. He'd never seen so much in his life, and it was all his.

He tried to look relaxed while the shop assistant counted the handful of bills, but he began to sweat when she tipped out his piggy bank and started sorting his entire life savings into neat piles of coins. Was it enough? He'd checked it at least five times, but…

The shop assistant gave Harvey a small, grey padded case with a picture of an armadillo on the front.

He felt his face growing hot. It was Monday, the day before the new school year started, and the shop was packed with people who'd do anything to own what Harvey was holding. He was sure they were all staring at him greedily.

"Th-thanks!" Harvey stammered, tucking the case safely under his arm and walking quickly from the shop. As soon as he was outside, he put his head down and sprinted towards home. He'd done it! He, Harvey Boots, had just bought a pair of Armadillo Aces, the best football cleats anyone could buy.

Skidding into Baker Street, he saw his neighbor, Professor Gertie, leaning from the top window of her inventing tower.

"Bring them up right away!"she called.

Harvey pushed open the door to the tower and clambered up the twisting stairs to where Mark 1, the Soccer Machine, was waiting. He was Professor Gertie's greatest invention: a robot designed purely for playing soccer.

Mark 1 grabbed for the Armadillo box, but Harvey held it out of his reach.

"Awww," Mark 1 complained, in his strange, mechanical voice.

"Over here!" Professor Gertie was at her workbench. "I know how hard you saved for those cleats," she said.

"It would be a terrible shame to get them scuffed and muddy your first game. So, especially for you, I've invented PAP. It stands for Polish And Protect."

She held up a sprayer Harvey had seen her use to water plants. Now it had skull-and-crossbones danger signs on it.

Harvey's hands tightened on his Armadillos. Professor Gertie's inventions sometimes backfired. "Er, have you tested it?" he asked politely.

Professor Gertie tutted. "What do you think?" She raised a foot and showed him one of her ancient white sandals. They were usually grubby, but now they shone so brightly it hurt Harvey to look at them.

Harvey wanted to feel encouraged, but he had the urge to escape. How could he though? Professor Gertie did everything she could for The Team. She'd invented Mark 1 for them and, as their coach, he'd helped them win the league last season, and a trip to Soccer Camp.

"Don't worry," Professor Gertie said soothingly. "PAP is designed to help, not harm."

With a *whirr*, Mark 1 tugged the case away from Harvey, unzipped it, and tipped the jet black Armadillo Aces onto the table. Professor Gertie lined them up in a patch of sunlight.

"They're magnificent!" she declared. "Now stand back…"

Mark 1 made an urgent blaring noise like a warning siren and dove behind the sofa.

Harvey didn't move. He couldn't take his eyes off the small Armadillo badges on the side of each boot. They looked so perfect…

Professor Gertie sprayed twice.

Harvey saw a rainbow through the mist of oily droplets. As each drop landed on the Aces, it left a wet, glistening spot. Harvey bent closer. The spots began to pop, sizzle and crack.

He jerked backwards as puffs of smoke erupted like tiny mushroom clouds. There was a smell like cheese and toilet cleaner and rotten fish. Harvey held his nose and looked pleadingly at Professor Gertie. She goggled despairingly back at him.

"But you said you'd tested it!" shouted Harvey, coughing as the boots steamed, writhed and shriveled into two shapeless black blobs.

"I did!" cried Professor Gertie, "As soon as I made it! Yesterday!"

She unscrewed the top of the plant sprayer, sniffed, then slumped down onto her stool.

"What is it?" asked Harvey. "What happened?"

"It's gone bad," she said feebly. "Oh, Harvey, what have I done?"

Chapter 2

"Where are they?" asked Darren as Harvey joined him and Rita on the field that evening. "You said you were getting Armadillos."

"Really?" asked Rita, surprised. "But how can Harvey afford those?"

Harvey looked longingly at Darren's and Rita's cleats. They both had new Power Strikes – not too expensive, but good enough. Harvey wished he'd bought the same ones, and not let Professor Gertie anywhere near them.

He sighed, and told Darren and Rita what had happened. Rita gave a short, shocked gasp. Darren hid his face behind his goalkeeper's gloves.

"Wait," Rita said, frowning. "I still don't understand…"

"They're gone!" Darren wailed. "Professor Gertie blew up Harvey's Armadillos!"

"Not that bit," said Rita, putting her hands on her hips. "How did you get a pair of Armadillo Aces in the first place?" she asked Harvey sternly.

Darren lowered his gloves. "He didn't steal them, if that's what you mean," he said. "Harvey bought them."

"Armadillos cost a fortune!" said Rita.

"I used my savings," said Harvey quickly.

"But how did you save enough…?" Rita began.

"He got money for his birthday," interrupted Darren. "And he spent what his folks gave him to buy new school stuff."

"I'll just wear my old uniform again," Harvey explained. "I'm sure it will still fit."

"It better," said Rita doubtfully, "And what about your old cleats? Do they still fit?"

She pointed at the well-worn Power
Juniors Harvey had on.

"They're a bit tight," admitted Harvey,
crouching down to loosen the laces as the
rest of The Team arrived. It was their first
meeting to plan for the new season, and
Harvey saw that everyone on The Team had
new cleats. Most wore Power Strikes, but not
Steffi. Her cleats were glittery lilac, Harvey
noticed, and they had "Primadonna"
scrawled along the side. She had a second,
bright pink pair dangling from one shoulder.

"I prefer not to wear the same color every game," Harvey heard her explain to Matt.

Matt lifted a foot, and Harvey felt a shiver run through him when he saw the tiny Armadillo badge. "Aces are as good as three pairs in one," Matt announced. Then he looked down at Harvey's cleats. "You should get professional ones like these, Harv. You'd score more goals, easy. I don't know why you're still wearing Juniors."

"They're so yesterday," commented Steffi, wrinkling her nose as if Harvey's old cleats smelled bad.

"They look like something out of a museum," agreed Matt.

"Harvey feels comfortable in them, that's all," said Darren defensively. "They're your lucky cleats, aren't they, Harvey?"

Harvey didn't want to explain, so he nodded.

"Is this supposed to be our lucky uniform, too?" asked Steffi, pouting as she tried to smooth the creases from her shirt.

"We look like we've just crawled out of a washing machine, and I feel crumply."

The Team were wearing shirts, shorts and socks made from Professor Gertie's Supercloth, which was supposed to never need washing. The problem was, Professor Gertie hadn't tested it with water, and when their uniforms got wet for the first time at Soccer Camp, The Team had been lost under a mountain of soap bubbles.

"Everyone makes mistakes," Harvey said gloomily. "Anyway, she rinsed out the soap, so we should be okay."

"I suppose we're stuck with them then," sulked Steffi.

The Team passed a ball around to warm up. Every time Harvey kicked it though, his squashed-up toes felt like they were being hit with a hammer. He tried a gentle flick to Rita, and winced in pain.

Howls of laughter came from the side of the field where, Harvey saw with dismay, a crowd had gathered to watch. He recognized several players from other teams, including the captain of the Diamonds, Paul Pepper, who was in his class at school.

"Keep trying!" Paul Pepper jeered. "Practice makes perfect!"

"What are they doing here?" asked Harvey.

"Checking us out," said Rita. "We're the team to beat this year. After all, last season we came from the bottom to make it to the top of the league."

Aware that he was being watched, Harvey kicked the ball high towards Matt, and then crumpled to the ground, rolling in agony.

"I heard something snap!" Harvey yelped, gripping his left cleat as he heard the spectators cheering. Then, closer to him, he heard someone chuckling.

"It's not funny!" Harvey told Rita through clenched teeth.

"Sorry!" Rita spluttered. "It's just…" She pointed at Harvey's foot and began laughing so hard she couldn't speak.

Harvey sat up, and saw that his big toe was waving in the air. It had poked clean through his cleat and his sock. "So that's what made the snapping sound," he said, sighing.

Matt crouched beside him. "If you can wiggle it, it's not broken," he said knowledgeably.

Harvey wiggled his toe. "It's okay," he said.

"Phew!" said Rita. "The last thing we need at the start of the season is an injured captain."

"What we really need is a captain with a decent pair of cleats," said Steffi glumly.

Harvey glanced from his useless Juniors to The Team's worried faces.

Then he blushed as, led by Paul Pepper, the audience on the sidelines began singing, "Boot up, boot up, Har-vey Boots!"

Harvey stayed seated on the grass. He didn't feel like getting up; things could only get worse. Then he saw that one of the people from the sidelines was walking towards him.

"That's Jackie Spoyle," whispered Rita. "Her dad owns Spoyle's Sports Shop. She goes to your school, doesn't she?"

Harvey nodded. He'd bought his Armadillos from Spoyle's, and Jackie had been there, choosing what she was now wearing: a black warm-up suit with soccer balls all over it.

"She lives in that big house on my street," Rita told him, "and she gets everything she wants. Last year it was her own gym to work out in. The year before she got a horse and jumps. She always gets the best gear, too."

"Looks like she's decided to be a soccer ball now," said Darren.

Harvey began to laugh, and then stopped. He'd just seen Jackie Spoyle's silver cleats. They had armadillos on the side, but they weren't Aces.

"These are Imps," Jackie told him. "They've only just come out and aren't even in the shops yet. But believe me, they're the best." She surveyed The Team, coughed lightly to clear her throat, and said, "I'm organizing a new squad of players. An elite squad."

It took Harvey a moment to realize what she meant, but before he could respond, Rita beat him to it. "You're not stealing anyone from The Team!" she said hotly.

"Get out of here!" snorted Matt, swatting the air as if he was shooing away a fly.

Jackie looked Matt up and down, making a face as if she'd tasted something nasty. "I will be hand-picking the most promising talent," she said. "Some of you will be hearing from me again. Others, alas, will not."

Matt cackled as she walked away, but Harvey noticed that Steffi was watching Jackie with interest. "It makes sense, when you think about it," Steffi muttered. "She's designing a team."

"Designer rubbish won't beat us," said Darren gruffly.

Harvey wasn't so sure. It all depended on who Jackie Spoyle could get to play for her – and what she had to attract them with.

Suddenly, Jackie spun around. "You do know you're all wrinkly, don't you?" she asked, smirking. "Anyone who joins me will have an all new uniform."

She unzipped her warm-up suit and Harvey heard his entire team gasp. Underneath, she was wearing a golden shirt, dazzling silver shorts and socks and, of course, the newest Armadillos.

Harvey couldn't take his eyes off them.

"Plus," Jackie continued, lifting one of her Imps to show off their gold-banded studs, "members of *my* team can choose anything else they need from my family's shop, for free."

Harvey heard a buzz of excitement, as if someone had stirred a beehive with a stick. Then someone called eagerly to Jackie, "What's your team called?"

"We're The Superteam," Jackie replied. "Didn't you know? You're playing us next Saturday…If The Team has any players left by then."

Chapter 3

"Look on the bright side," said Steffi. "Quality opposition means The Team will have to play better. It'll be good for us."

"But she wants to steal our players!" said Darren.

"And our name," said Harvey. "She's just putting 'super' in front of it, that's all."

"Jackie Spoyle might always get what she wants," said Rita, "but she's not getting The Team!" She snatched the ball from Matt and angrily kicked it into the air.

There was a silence, followed by a loud gong that sounded like someone had hit a trashcan with a baseball bat. Harvey turned and saw Mark 1 rubbing his head as he bounded over, his eyes flashing.

The robot put a powerful hand on Harvey's shoulder and began dragging him away. "Mine!" he bleated urgently. "MINE!"

Harvey jogged along beside Mark 1, trying not to catch his big toe in the grass, or stub it on the pavement. Darren and Rita followed behind.

"What's wrong?" Harvey kept asking, but Mark 1 didn't reply.

When they reached Baker Street, Harvey increased his pace. Something was going on at the inventing tower. As they drew closer, he saw a sign:

"For Sale! Amazing Inventions!"

Professor Gertie trudged from the tower door, her arms full of strange and wonderful-looking objects which she dropped with a crash onto her lawn.

Harvey heard Mark 1 start to tick rapidly, like a bomb about to go off.

"Have no fear!" Professor Gertie said when she spotted them. "By this time tomorrow, Harvey will be ankle-deep in Armadillos!"

Darren squatted down and grabbed an invention. It was the Shoosh! Gun that Harvey had seen Professor Gertie use to shoot nets over spiders. Rita poked delicately at some portable Lock Jaws, which were a new kind of safe.

"You won't have any problem selling these!" Darren said. "It's the first day of school tomorrow and nearly everyone walks past here."

"Do they really?" Professor Gertie asked, giving Harvey a knowing wink.

With a distressed *beep!*, Mark 1 let go of Harvey's arm, scooped up as many things as he could from the ground, and disappeared inside the tower with them. Harvey heard him clattering up the stairs at top speed.

Professor Gertie sighed loudly. "For some reason, that robot thinks all my useless gadgets belong to him. His bedroom is packed full of them!"

"You mean these are all Mark 1's?" asked Rita.

"Don't worry," said Professor Gertie. "There's nothing here of any real value."

Harvey couldn't believe what he was hearing. "I'm not having any cleats bought with Mark 1's stuff!" he said, looking to Rita and Darren for support.

"It's totally unfair," agreed Rita. "But then again…" she bit her lip. "We won't beat The Superteam if you have to play in your socks, will we?"

"You're our captain," said Darren firmly. "If you can't play your best, The Team won't hold together. You need cleats, Harvey."

"And I ruined your Armadillos," said Professor Gertie. "So you have to let me buy you another pair."

Harvey shook his head, but didn't say anything.

"To tell you the truth," Professor Gertie said brightly, "I'm quite enjoying myself. It's about time my inventions started earning me some cash!"

She skipped merrily back inside the tower.

"Mark 1 shouldn't have to suffer," Harvey told Darren and Rita. "If there were any other way of getting new cleats, I'd take it."

"Well, there is one possibility," said Rita. "You could borrow Steffi's spare pair."

Darren was aghast. "But they're pink!"

Rita retreated down Baker Street, pulling Darren along with her.

"Pink cleats are better than no cleats," Rita insisted.

"Don't do it, Harvey!" Darren cried.

Darren was right, Harvey thought. There was no way his reputation would survive if he was seen wearing pink cleats.

That night, Harvey stayed up late, watching through his bedroom window as Professor Gertie carried inventions from her tower, and Mark 1 bundled them straight back inside again. The robot was now making furious popping noises and giving off steam.

Then, around ten o'clock, Harvey heard a high-pitched *BEEEEeeeeeeeep!* followed by silence. Mark 1 didn't emerge from the tower again.

Harvey felt uneasy as he crawled into bed and began rubbing his sore toes. He didn't know what he was going to do. The Team needed him, but so did Mark 1.

As he drifted off to sleep, he was only sure of one thing – he would stand and face The Superteam on Saturday, even if he had to play barefoot. Nobody was going to take over The Team.

Chapter 4

A girl was shrieking, "I'm having it, and there's nothing you can do about it!"

Harvey's eyes snapped open. Darting to his window, he saw that it was morning, and Professor Gertie's Amazing Inventions Sale was in full swing.

Harvey hurriedly searched for the pants and sweater he'd worn to school last year, and tugged them on. Everything felt tight and short, and he couldn't even get his shoes on his feet until he had loosened the laces as far as they would go.

"One at a time!" he heard Professor Gertie holler. "If you fight over them, you'll break them!"

Harvey left his house at full speed and jumped over the fence into Professor Gertie's garden. He dodged a group of small boys who were stuck together with Velcro Balls, and spotted Professor Gertie sitting at a table facing a long line of shoppers.

Harvey groaned. He was too late. Nearly all her inventions had sold already. He looked around for Mark 1, but couldn't see him.

A girl next to him held up a pile of paper. "What's this?" she asked.

"Aha," said Professor Gertie. "That's my Rub-a-Dub paper!"

Harvey watched her press a piece of the plain paper onto her open notebook. When she peeled it off, she'd made an exact copy.

"It's for homework!" the girl squealed. Professor Gertie began to sell the Rub-a-Dub paper one sheet at a time.

Darren arrived, looking pleased. "At this rate she'll have the money to buy your cleats in no time," said Darren. "Come on, we're late."

As they walked down the hill, Harvey felt cool air around his wrists and ankles. He tried pulling his sleeves down, but they sprang back up again. Then, as they turned into the school grounds, he was met by a chorus of giggling girls. Jackie Spoyle was standing with her friends, blocking the path.

"Look everyone," said Jackie. "This year Harvey Boots is setting the style!"

Harvey blushed as Jackie's gang shrieked with laughter.

Darren barged through them, making a gap so that Harvey could follow.

"Steffi says Harvey *likes* old things," Jackie went on. "He doesn't look very comfortable in them though!"

Darren turned on her. "What have you been talking to Steffi for?"

"I've been chatting to all the league's stars," Jackie said primly. "I do wish Steffi went to our school. She's got the right kind of attitude, doesn't she? And Rita, too, she's *very* keen."

Darren's face turned fiery red, but before he could say anything else, Harvey hustled him into their classroom. "Forget about it," Harvey said. "Rita would never play for her."

Darren collapsed onto a chair at the back of the class. "Maybe not," he said. "But some of the others might. Steffi's always complaining that we don't have a cool uniform. She'll be the first to go."

Throughout the morning, Harvey and Darren tried to work out who would be tempted to join The Superteam. They had plenty of time to talk. Their teacher, Mr. Spottiwoode, was trying to keep the class from rioting.

"I hope Professor Gertie doesn't get into trouble for this," Harvey said as a boy near them used the Shoosh! Gun to fire nets over himself until his hair looked like it was covered in thick, stringy cobwebs.

Darren was batting away bubbles. "Where are these coming from?" he asked. One burst over him. "Hey! They stink!"

"It must be Professor Gertie's Blow Off," Harvey explained. "It captures smells inside bubbles. Rekha's using it."

By the end of the day, Mr. Spottiwoode's desk was piled high with confiscated inventions, and Darren was busy scribbling a list of all the players The Team were likely to lose.

He showed it to Harvey on their way home.

"You've written down everyone but me and you!" said Harvey.

"We're the only ones I can be absolutely sure of," said Darren.

"What about Rita?"

Darren grimaced. "We can't be certain…"

"Yes, we can," said Harvey, and he scratched off Rita's name. Then he noticed a large crowd gathered around Professor Gertie's tower.

"What's going on?" he asked, breaking into a run. "I thought she sold everything this morning."

Darren jumped up to see over people's heads. "Looks like she's found a few tons more. Mark 1's bedroom must have been jam-packed!"

They pushed their way through, and found Professor Gertie weighing an ancient handbag in her hands. It made a dull rattle just like the sound Harvey's piggy bank had made when it was full.

Professor Gertie waved when she saw Harvey. "If I keep my sale going all week, we should have enough money for your cleats by Friday."

"All week?" asked Harvey dismally. "How many more inventions do you have left to sell?"

"Thousands," purred Professor Gertie, rubbing her hands together.

"How's Mark 1?" Harvey asked hopefully. "Is he feeling better?"

"He won't get out of bed," said Professor Gertie. "He normally only does that when he's thinking very hard, but this time he seems to have turned himself off!"

Harvey felt terrible. Mark 1 had never turned himself off before! Harvey had to tell Professor Gertie to stop the sale. There was no way he could accept cleats bought in this way.

"I'm not…" he started to say, and then he was knocked off his feet as a crush of shoppers suddenly surged forward.

He just had time to see someone holding up what looked like a hard hat with helicopter blades before he crawled away on his hands and knees.

"I've got an idea," Darren said excitedly as Harvey stood up. "The Team's practice sessions are always on Thursday nights, right?"

"Yeah," Harvey sighed, "so what?"

"So, the people who turn up on Thursday will see that The Team's captain still doesn't have cleats, and they might decide to join Spoyle's team after all."

"There's nothing we can do about it,"
said Harvey.

"There is," said Darren. "I'll call everyone
and change the practice session to Friday."
He grinned. "When they see your Armadillos,
there's no way they'll give up on The Team!"

As he watched Darren jog home, Harvey
felt his own energy drain away. He slouched
into his house and up to his room.

"I'm not going to wear Professor Gertie's
Armadillos," he decided finally.

There had to be some other way of
keeping The Team together. Harvey curled up
in bed and began to think very hard.

He was soon snoring noisily.

Chapter 5

The rest of the week seemed to Harvey like a game everyone else was playing while he sat on the sidelines and watched.

On Wednesday, Professor Gertie's sale was busier than the day before, Jackie and her friends welcomed him to school with a well-practiced cheer, Darren talked constantly about the new Armadillos Harvey would be getting, and Mr. Spottiwoode spent the whole day pouncing on Professor Gertie's inventions.

On Thursday morning, the sale was still busy; Jackie and her friends applauded Harvey when he arrived at school, and Mr. Spottiwoode lost part of his moustache when a hungry Frizz Bee landed on his nose.

"They're for trimming knotted bits of hair, actually," Harvey heard Rekha explain to her friend, "definitely not for moustaches."

Harvey's spirits rose briefly on Thursday afternoon.

He scored with one of his best-ever
swerving free kicks on the playground, and
Jackie Spoyle was watching.

"That will give her something to think
about!" Darren shouted, adding to Harvey,
"You'll be unstoppable once you've got your
Armadillos."

At last, on Friday morning, Harvey began
to feel some relief. Professor Gertie, who
looked exhausted, was no longer bringing
out more inventions from her tower. And
when Harvey got to school, Jackie and her
friends were nowhere in sight.

"When Spoyle saw you score yesterday, she got worried," Darren reported later that afternoon. "She's now promising The Superteam free tickets to professional games, a real soccer coach, and an all-expenses-paid international summer tournament!"

Harvey felt like he'd been kicked in the stomach. "How can we compete with that?" he asked despairingly.

"Easy," said Darren. "First, you get your Armadillos. That will help most of The Team decide to stay with us. Then we hammer The Superteam into the ground."

Harvey saw a triumphant glint in Darren's eyes, and knew he was going to let his friend down badly. He wouldn't be wearing Armadillos, and it was about time he told Darren.

Suddenly, Harvey heard a long, agonized scream, and saw Paul Pepper waving his hand violently in the air, trying to dislodge a pair of Lock Jaws.

"What on earth is that?" demanded Mr. Spottiwoode.

"I keep my pencils in it," said the shy boy who sat next to Paul Pepper. He keyed a code into the base of the Lock Jaw, and Paul Pepper's hand was released. "I bought it from the professor who lives next door to Harvey Boots," the boy said. "That's where *all* these weird things come from."

The bell began to ring for the end of the day, and Harvey and Darren ducked their heads and bolted from the room. "Let's get the money, then go to Spoyle's to buy your Armadillos," urged Darren.

They ran through the school gates and onto Baker Street where Harvey tugged on Darren's arm to make him stop. "I can't do it," he said. "That money belongs to Mark 1, and he should have it."

Harvey looked into his friend's face, expecting Darren to be devastated, or at least upset. But to his surprise, Darren smiled with satisfaction.

"Brilliant idea!" he said, blinking rapidly as he worked it out. "Mark 1 gets the cash, and then we ask him to do what he was invented for: saving The Team."

Harvey was confused. Had Darren forgotten? "The referees won't let robots play," Harvey reminded him.

Darren shook his head. "I didn't mean that. All Mark 1 has to do is buy you some Armadillos!"

Harvey thought about it and began to feel excited. Of course Mark 1 would want to help them! "Let Mark 1 choose what to do," Harvey decided.

"If he wants to get me some cleats, I'll wear them. But I'll pay him back. I don't care how long it takes. I could even buy back some of Professor Gertie's inventions for him…"

Darren sneezed. "What's that smell?"

Harvey sniffed, and the memory of melting Armadillos came back to him like a nightmare he couldn't forget. He glanced up and saw a wisp of smoke rising from beside the inventing tower.

They found Professor Gertie standing in her garden, as still as a statue, holding the plant sprayer with the skull-and-crossbones stickers. On the path next to her, a pair of Armadillo Aces were on fire.

"I made it fresh," she said weakly, giving the sprayer a tiny shake. "I decided to buy your cleats for you as a surprise, and I was rushing to have them ready and...Oh, Harvey, I must have made a mistake when I mixed the formula!"

"Not again!" said Darren. "Wait a minute, how much of the money did you spend?"

"*All* of it!" whimpered Professor Gertie.

"There's nothing else we can do then," said Darren, holding his head in his hands. "I give up!"

Chapter 6

Harvey and Darren met Rita on the field that night. While they waited for the others to arrive, Darren told her about the new Armadillos.

"I know that Professor Gertie means well," Rita said, speaking very, very quietly. "But sometimes," she said, her voice rising, "I wish she would stop trying to MAKE THINGS BETTER!"

"Me too," said Harvey.

"Me three," said Darren grumpily.

"And where is everyone?" Rita snapped, when it was clear that nobody else was going to turn up. "I thought Matt would stay with us, at least."

"You did tell everyone that the practice session had changed to tonight, didn't you?" Harvey checked with Darren.

Darren slapped his forehead with his gloved hand.

"You mean you didn't?!" cried Rita. "But hang on, you told *me*!"

"I was too busy persuading the others not to join The Superteam!" said Darren. "I just forgot!"

"But that means that anyone else who wanted to stay on The Team would have shown up *yesterday*!" cried Rita.

"And because we weren't there," said Harvey, "they'll think we've joined Jackie's team. So they'll probably join too!"

Friday night practice was over.

It was dark when Harvey arrived home.
Someone was waiting outside his house.

"Here's what you need," said Jackie
Spoyle.

Harvey could barely see what she was
giving him, but he knew the feel of
Armadillos as he held them in his hands.
And these weren't Aces. They were lighter,
and more supple, and...

"They're your size," said Jackie. "I'm
captain of The Superteam – but tomorrow,
you can be our striker."

Harvey didn't hear her leave. He was busy
getting used to his Imps.

Chapter 7

Harvey left his house on a cloudy Saturday morning carrying a shopping bag.

"You were right, and I was wrong," said Professor Gertie, who was trying to fix her trampled flowerbeds. "I should never have taken away Mark 1's things. He won't come out of his room, or let me in, and I know he's up to something in there."

"You did what you thought was best," said Harvey.

Professor Gertie wasn't listening to him. "I wish I could give his things back. There *is* one thing I didn't sell." She pointed to a shadow behind the tower door.

Harvey took a step closer to see what it was, then cringed. Icy shivers ran up and down his spine.

It was Masher, the monstrous waste disposal machine that Professor Gertie had made to eat inventions that didn't work.

Harvey once had a nightmare where Masher was trying to catch him. Now, looking into the killer machine's beady eyes, he wondered if he really had been dreaming. Its rows of jagged teeth were gnawing on the chain that secured it to a metal ring on the wall, and its crab-like claw was nipping chunks out of a sign that said:

"*Weird Pet For Sale! (Pat him, he's friendly!)*"

"Y-you've got to be joking!" spluttered Harvey.

"People are always on the look-out for something different," said Professor Gertie. "And Masher would make an ideal family companion. He likes children; he only needs oiling once a week, and he eats any old junk."

Harvey eyed Masher warily, as he would a dog that was known to bite. A noise like stones being crushed came from deep inside the creature's mechanical jaws.

"His growl is worse than his bite," said Professor Gertie. "His teeth are worn down, and his claw is blunt, the poor dear."

Harvey was about to tell Professor Gertie that she couldn't let Masher loose on innocent people, when he realized he had nothing to worry about. There was no way anybody would want Masher.

"I have to go," said Harvey. "And don't worry about my cleats anymore; it's taken care of."

When he reached the field, Harvey saw The Team mingling with about twenty other players. He recognized most of them; they were nearly all the league's best goal scorers.

Jackie hadn't picked a single defender, and Harvey guessed that The Superteam defense was going to be useless.

He spotted Jackie modeling The Superteam's gold and silver uniform. Behind her there was a neat pile of Armadillo boxes. The Superteam players were going to be equipped with the finest of everything, just as Jackie had promised.

Harvey strolled up to her.

"Hi, Striker," said Jackie. "I'm glad you're with us." She unfolded a golden shirt and draped it over his shoulders. "This is for you," she said, beaming.

Harvey lifted the Imps from his bag. He saw Darren and Rita standing side by side, with their mouths open in disbelief.

"No thanks," Harvey said to Jackie. "I have a team already. These are for you."

Jackie's smile vanished as he gave her back the Imps. She snatched back the shirt. "You *lose*, Harvey Boots," she spat after him as he turned his back on her. "You've already *lost*."

Harvey, Darren and Rita headed arm in arm towards the field. Harvey's heart was thumping. This was it. If the rest of The Team didn't follow, they really would have lost before the game even started.

Steffi strode past them. "Come on," she said angrily, "let's show Superbrat what a *real* team can do!"

Matt trotted closely behind her. "Poor Steffi!" he said quietly. "She wasn't part of Spoiled's designs; she was only asked to be their *substitute*!"

Harvey watched with pride as The Team took their positions on the field.

"I don't get it," said Darren. "Everyone is here!"

"Of course they are," said Rita. "We're The Team, remember? Teams are teams because they stick together, no matter what."

Harvey, though, noticed that some of his teammates were frowning at his well-worn school shoes.

"These are fine," he told everyone. "I play in them every day."

"On grass?" asked Steffi.

"No," said Harvey, "but…"

"In the rain?" asked Steffi as a dark cloud bathed them in shadow.

Harvey didn't answer her. "If it rains," he muttered to Rita, "my shoes are going to slide all over the place."

"It won't rain," Rita said confidently.

The teams faced each other. The Superteam team members who weren't playing this time stood on the sidelines wearing golden baseball caps and chanting their support.

The referee blew her whistle, and Harvey kicked off, just as a cold drop of rain landed on his nose.

"That cloud doesn't have more than an eggcup of rain in it," said Rita carelessly as she returned the ball to him.

Heavy drops began falling on Harvey's head. He back-heeled the ball to Steffi, then ran into the empty space to receive it.

But as he reached out his left leg, his
right foot slipped, tumbling him to the grass.
Rita gathered the ball and headed for The
Superteam's goal. Harvey could hardly see
her through the downpour, and the next
thing he knew, a Superteam player was trying
to set up an attack.

Harvey closed in on her fast, stuck out his
foot to intercept the ball, then skidded,
tripped and dove headfirst into her stomach,
knocking her flat on her back.

The ref stood over Harvey, showing him a
yellow card. "Outrageous foul!" she said
furiously. "One more like that and I'm
sending you off!"

Harvey slipped twice more as he limped to the side of the field. The rain was stopping, but the grass was already soaked and muddy.

"Keep out of the action until it dries," Rita advised him.

Harvey watched helplessly as the game went on in front of him. His absence was putting The Team under pressure, but Harvey was encouraged by how they responded.

Rita dropped back into defense, and they built their forward moves slowly so that The Superteam couldn't break through them on the counterattack. The problem was, The Team were unable to finish their attacks; without Harvey, they didn't have a natural goal-scorer, but The Superteam had plenty.

Harvey watched Paul Pepper gather the ball and set a straight course for Darren's goal, skipping past one Team player after another.

"Tackle him!" Harvey bellowed. Matt, Steffi and Rita lunged for the ball, but Paul Pepper still managed to shoot.

Darren dove at full stretch, pushed the ball onto the post with his fingertips, and slid along the grass, leaving the goal undefended. Harvey put up his arms to celebrate the save, and then saw Jackie trot up to the ball. All she had to do was walk it into the net, and with a grin of triumph, she did.

Harvey watched in frustration as Jackie Spoyle did a victory dance in front of him. He felt desperate. He had to play somehow.

Then he saw Mark 1 racing across the field, balancing a tattered picnic basket on his head and calling urgently, "Cleeeeets!"

Chapter 8

Mark 1 set the picnic basket on the
ground, and Harvey rummaged through a
jumbled mass of string, a sink plunger,
yogurt cups with smiley faces painted on the
sides, old corks, a tea strainer, and two egg
cartons packed with grey powder.

"Is there something here for me?" Harvey
asked.

"Cleeeeets!!" said the robot, nodding
happily.

Harvey searched again. He heard The
Superteam cheer as they scored a second
goal, and he began to panic. "Where are
they?" he asked anxiously. "Which cleats?"

Mark 1 bent down and unraveled the
strung-together objects. Then he wrapped
them around Harvey's shoes. He pulled the
strings tight, tied a complicated knot, and
held Harvey's hand as he tried to balance on
the wobbly egg cartons.

Harvey didn't know what to say. The Superteam were celebrating their third goal, and he was standing on trash.

He took a step. After all, he told himself, Mark 1 had made them for him. The least he could do was try them.

Mark 1 shoved him onto the field just as the ball came bouncing their way.

Harvey took huge strides towards it. Concentrating on not falling over, he didn't hear the whistle for halftime. Instead, he lined himself up to kick the ball, drew back his left foot, and…the egg cartons exploded.

"Aaargh!" cried Harvey as he flew into the air, flapped his arms wildly, and crashed to the ground.

The Team wandered over as Harvey kicked off his burning shoes. Mark 1 snatched them up, tutting as he examined them.

"Looks like I'm playing in my bare feet," said Harvey as he quickly rolled off his smoldering socks.

A pair of pink Primadonnas fell into his lap. He looked up to see Steffi's embarrassed but determined face. "It's our only chance," she said.

Harvey heard The Superteam and their supporters start chanting, "Boot up, boot up, Har-vey Boots!" Jackie was laughing so hard her teeth reminded him of Professor Gertie's Lock Jaws.

"Don't even think about it," Darren warned, shaking his finger at Steffi's cleats as if he were scolding them. "Just…don't."

But Harvey knew it was their only hope. He put them on, stood up, and saw Professor Gertie marching towards him, holding a Spoyle Sports shoe box.

"No!" Harvey exclaimed, feeling like everything around him was going wrong, wrong, wrong. "You can't have sold Masher!"

"Even better than that," said Professor Gertie.

"But he's *dangerous!*" Harvey roared.

"Mr. Spotty? Oh, I wouldn't say he was *that* bad," said Professor Gertie in surprise.

"Mr. Spotty?" Harvey asked, bewildered.

"Your *teacher*," explained Professor Gertie.

"Mr. Spottiwoode bought Masher?" asked Darren.

"Of course he didn't," said Professor Gertie. "He came to ask about my inventions."

"Are you in trouble?" Harvey asked seriously.

"Quite the opposite," said Professor Gertie. "Your wonderful Mr. Spotty wants to buy thirty Lock Jaws!"

"What does he want those for?" asked Darren.

"He wants everyone in his class to have a secure pencil case," said the Professor. "Mr. Spotty said he'll be able to start his lessons on time if he doesn't have to find all the lost pencils and pens first."

"And he *paid* you for them?" asked Darren in astonishment.

"Yes!" cried Professor Gertie delightedly. "Although," she continued, "he only gave me a little bit to start with, and it wasn't enough to buy the cleats you wanted, Harvey. I could only afford the cheapest pair."

"*Any* will do," said Harvey with relief as Professor Gertie handed him a pair of ordinary black cleats.

"Don't worry," the professor said, leaning close so that only Harvey could hear.

"I stopped by the tower on the way here and fixed them up a bit."

Harvey groaned and hung his head, wishing that, just for once, Professor Gertie wouldn't interfere. Everything she'd invented for him lately had been a disaster.

"Aren't you going to try them?" she asked.

Harvey shrugged. He put on the new cleats carefully, handed Steffi back her Primadonnas, and walked to the edge of the center circle, taking small, delicate steps.

His feet felt cool and airy. Without thinking, he bounced up and down to get ready, then stopped. His toes had begun to tingle.

"Are you all right?" asked Rita. "You look scared!"

Harvey didn't reply. He heard the ref blow her whistle to start the second half, and felt his body tense up expectantly. He had no idea what would happen next.

Chapter 9

The Superteam kicked off and Rita chased for the ball. Harvey didn't move. His feet had suddenly become warm.

"Move it, Harvey!" called Matt, threading the ball to him. Harvey automatically took a step forward and intercepted it, feeling his cleats respond just like ordinary cleats should. The only difference was that these were so snug they felt like his feet's second skin.

Harvey was too nervous to kick the ball, so he used the side of his foot to roll it back to Steffi, and was surprised to see that it arrived exactly where he'd intended. Seeing a gap, he burst through, collected the ball on the run and stroked it gently ahead of him. Now he had a chance for a long shot.

"Shoot!" yelled Professor Gertie.

Harvey slowed down, waiting for his cleats to do something they shouldn't. What *had* Professor Gertie done to them?

He nudged the ball again. Nothing happened. The Superteam defenders were closing in, but he still had time to shoot. If only Professor Gertie's inventions didn't *always* catch fire, or blow up, or melt or just not work.

Well, some of the time her ideas *almost* worked…

"SHOOOOT!" insisted Mark 1.

With a mighty yell, Harvey put his trust in Professor Gertie.

He blasted the ball towards The Superteam's goal, watching it take off like a missile, skimming the grass, and spinning to the left. The goalkeeper dove low and got both hands to it, but he couldn't stop it.

"Goal!"

As the rest of The Team and their two supporters celebrated, Harvey took a close look at his left cleat. It still looked normal. "I don't believe it," he said, confused.

"Neither do I," said the ref suspiciously, pressing Harvey's cleat with her thumbs. "You haven't got a lump of steel in here, have you?"

"I dunno," said Harvey. "I mean, no, they're not heavy."

The ref examined his other cleat before restarting the game.

They felt alive, a part of him that did whatever he wanted them to do. He couldn't imagine what Professor Gertie had done to them, but he was sure of one thing; this time, her invention was a spectacular success.

Harvey sailed in a cross, and Rita
thundered the ball into the net with her
head. "Goal!"

Harvey did a back flip that fooled The
Superteam defense, leaving the way open for
Matt to trickle the ball home. "Goal!"

Harvey sent the ball curling from a free
kick for his second goal, and soon after made
his hat trick directly from a corner kick.
"Goal! Goal!"

"Am I dreaming?" asked Darren, snatching off a glove so he could pinch himself.

"This is pathetic!" Harvey heard Paul Pepper whine as Steffi headed the ball through the goalie's legs. "You call this a super team? We might as well give up."

Other players from Jackie's team nodded their heads in agreement.

"Play on!" Jackie ordered. "I say when we give up!"

Harvey put his foot on the ball and watched as Paul Pepper wrenched off his top and threw it at her. "I don't like your style!" he hollered. "This isn't a team at all!"

"I know it's a bit early," said the ref hurriedly, "but we might as well call it a day." She blew the final whistle and said, "The Team wins six to three!"

Harvey tore down the field with his arms in the air and saw Darren staring at him with a look of terror on his face.

"What's wro-" Harvey began. Then, he heard the sound of grinding metal behind him. He spun around.

Masher's feet were pounding deep holes in the grass as he came at Harvey, teeth whizzing like chainsaws, claw snapping, and bitten-through chain whipping the air.

Harvey dove out of the way, rolled onto his knees, and looked around. Masher continued past him across the field, with Professor Gertie trailing behind.

"Mashy!" she cooed gently, "Here, Mashy!"

Masher reached The Superteam, his eyes rocking back and forth as if looking for someone. Harvey heard Paul Pepper bellow, "Your Superteam are JUNK!"

Suddenly, Masher darted forward. Jackie screamed as the metal monster pinched off one of her Armadillo Imps with his claw. Still screaming, she sprinted across the field.

Rita giggled. "Looks like Mashy's got the munchies!"

"But why did he pick on Spoyle?" asked Darren.

"Because," laughed Harvey, "he eats any old junk!"

Professor Gertie dashed after Masher and pulled him back by his chain. Then she gave Mark 1 a one-armed hug.

"That means sorry," she said. "From now on, anything I make that doesn't work is yours forever."

"He'll need an aircraft hanger to store it all," said Darren under his breath.

Professor Gertie put Masher's chain into Mark 1's hand and asked, "How would you like a weird pet?"

The robot's eyes flickered as he bent down to stroke the wire bristles on Masher's back. Masher made a purring noise, and Harvey covered his ears. The sound was horrible.

"Professor Gertie, what did you do to Harvey's cleats?" Rita wanted to know. "I mean, they were fantastic!"

"*Harvey* was fantastic," said Professor Gertie, prying off Harvey's left cleat. "All I did was…this!"

She pulled out a big wad of cotton balls. "They didn't have these cleats in Harvey's size," she explained, "so I had to stuff the toes to make them fit."

Harvey gasped. "Is that *all*? I thought…"

Professor Gertie smiled. "You didn't think I was going to let you down, did you?" she asked innocently.

Harvey looked around. Darren and Rita were always with him, of course. But so were the rest of The Team, and that included Mark 1 and Professor Gertie. They stuck together, no matter what.

Harvey grinned at Professor Gertie. "You? Let me down?" He started to laugh. "Never!"

Professor
Gertie

Darren

Harvey

Rita

Matt

Steffi

Mark 1